Richard Heber Newton

The Children's Church

A Service book and hymnal for use in the Sunday-school and Church

Richard Heber Newton

The Children's Church
A Service book and hymnal for use in the Sunday-school and Church

ISBN/EAN: 9783744755399

Printed in Europe, USA, Canada, Australia, Japan

Cover: Foto ©Lupo / pixelio.de

More available books at **www.hansebooks.com**

THE
CHILDREN'S CHURCH:

A

SERVICE BOOK AND HYMNAL

FOR

USE IN THE

SUNDAY-SCHOOL AND CHURCH

BY R. HEBER NEWTON.

NEW YORK:

ANSON D. F. RANDOLPH & CO.,

770 BROADWAY, COR. OF NINTH ST.

PREFACE.

THIS book is the unexpected outgrowth of an attempt to supply my own Sunday-school with a carefully-made Selection of Hymns, a Liturgy for use in the School, and the Service for the Children's Church, combined in one volume. In the hope that a like want, felt doubtless by others, may be partially met by it, the book is made public.

The opening and closing exercises of the Sunday-school are based upon the OFFICES OF DEVOTION, prepared by the *Rev. Richard Newton, D.D.*, and approved by extensive use through a number of years.

The Service of *the Children's Church,* now coming to be so happily customary, is found in the ORDER FOR EVENING PRAYER, *arranged as used;* the Psalter (a portion of the Selections of Psalms) being inserted in its proper position, thus simplifying the children's use of the service.

Five of the authorized Selections of Psalms are given; enough to meet the hoped-for introduction of the Children's Church into the regular Sunday services.

Special Anthems and Canticles are added, for use on Festival-days and other occasions, as may be desired, and as may be proper in each case. The Anthem for Epiphany Sunday, the Gloria Christi, and the Beatitudes, are from the Directory for the use of the Prayer-book in St. Johnland, issued by the Rev. Dr. Muhlenberg; the others are from the Prayer-book.

The Psalter is pointed for chaunting, experience showing that this is the true rendering for children. This will not interfere with its use in reading where so desired.

The bars before every alternate versicle are to aid the eye in antiphonal chaunting

The pointing of the Psalter, and of the Canticles and Anthems, is that of the Trinity Church Psalter (Dr. Cutler's).

Of the third and chief part, THE HYM-NAL, it may properly be said that it is no hasty compilation, but the result of a long and pains-taking examination of a large number of hymn-books.

More than half the hymns are from the Hymnal authorized by the late General Convention. Children are worthy of something better than the wretched doggerel, unhealthy in sentiment, vapid in meaning, which is palmed off upon our schools as specially adapted to their capacities. They ought to have words worthy of being impressed by music abidingly on the memory. In some hymns slight verbal changes have been made to render their sentiment truthful in children's lips.

The hymns taken from " The Hymnal ' have their number designated, and thus, where desired, the singing in the Children's

Church Service can be confined to those hymns, and the church hymnals can be used by the congregation.

Reference is made for music to a number of books in general use. Music swells greatly the size and cost of a Hymnal, and is only a confusion to children.

In publishing a music-book, tunes have to be manufactured for a large proportion of the hymns—with the usual result of muse-work made to order—inferiority.

By referring for tunes to different music-books, a wide range of choice is afforded, and none but good music need be used.

Beyond such a modest contribution to the improvement of Sunday-school music, as a selection from the tunes now in favor—and thus in accord with the actual attainment of taste—this book could not have ventured. The lack of any ability for a higher task, and the lack of faith in any other than gradual education, alike limited the aim of this hymnal.

The Musical Index at the end of the book gives the reference for the music of each hymn. As that index refers to all the books in the reference list in which each tune is found, the necessity of multiplying copies is avoided as far as possible.

A List of the music-books in the order of their importance (for the use of this book) precedes the index.

A few special arrangements for some of the hymns have been thrown into the form of a " *Supplement*," to which reference is duly made. The music of the Supplement has been supervised for the press by Mr. Samuel Jackson.

Both by the title chosen for this book, and by the underlying provision in its plan, it is evident that one hope I have had in it, is that it may facilitate the introduction of the CHILDREN'S CHURCH as a regular service of the Lord's Day, wherein the inadequacy of our Sunday-school instruction, and the lamentable neglect of home education, may be supplemented by a service of worship in the church, with a systematic course of pulpit teaching from the pastor.

It only remains to add my grateful acknowledgement of help rendered and courtesies extended in this work: by A. E. G. in the arrangement of most of the music in *the Supplement*, and in the general selection of tunes; by Mr. Francis Wells in the same task of selection, and in the contribution of words and music; by Mrs. Lewis Thatcher in the use of music composed by the late Mr. Lewis Thatcher; by Mr. George Weeks in the use of words and music; by Messrs. C. K. Fay, W. A. Farr, Charles Wels, and Samuel Jackson, in the contribution of tunes, and by Mr. Jackson in other valuable services; and lastly, by the authors and publishers of the copyrighted hymns named below, in the favour of their use.

R. Heber Newton.

September, 1872.

COPYRIGHTED HYMNS

USED IN THIS BOOK BY PERMISSION.

———◆———

From "FRESH LAURELS." Messrs. Biglow & Main, Publishers, New York.

Jesus is our living Saviour.

From "CLARIONA." Biglow & Main.

There is beauty all around.
Sweet the Sabbath morning.

From "SONGS OF GLADNESS." J. C. Garrigues & Co., Phila

Sitting at the feet of Jesus.
Marching on ! marching on ! glad as birds on the wing.
My Saviour stands waiting, and knocks at the door.
What shall I do with Jesus ?

From "HAPPY VOICES." American Tract Society, N. Y.

O won't you be a Christian while you 're young.
The city's hum is hush'd and still.
He is risen, He is not here.

From "THE CHAPLET." Harrison Millard, New York.

Blessed is He that cometh.
Fight the good fight bravely.
Through the day so rosy bright.
Christ is risen ! Christ is risen !

CONTENTS

III.—HYMNAL. TABLE OF SUBJECTS.

CONTENTS. xiii

ORDER.

Opening School.

1. HYMN: All standing.
2. RESPONSIVE SCRIPTURE SELECTIONS.
   Season or Topic and Page announced.
3. GLORIA PATRI.
4. [CREED.]
5. PRAYER: All kneeling.
6. [THE LESSON OF THE DAY IN THE SCHOOL, OR THE GOSPEL OF THE DAY.]   Read by Superintendent, scholars seated.
7. HYMN OR CHANT: Standing.

Closing School.

1. HYMN: Standing.
2. NOTICES, ETC.   Scholars seated.
3. [RECITATION OF THE LESSON.]
4. SUMMING UP OF THE LESSON, OR ADDRESS by Rector or Superintendent.
5. [HYMN:]   Standing.
6. PRAYER: All kneeling.

Responsive Scripture Selections

FOR THE SEASONS OF THE CHURCH YEAR.

ADVENT.

Superintendent. The voice of him that crieth in the wilderness, Prepare ye the way of the Lord; make straight in the desert a highway for our God.

Scholars. The glory of the Lord shall be revealed, and all flesh shall see it together; for the mouth of the Lord hath spoken it. —Isa. xl. 3, 5.

Sup. Rejoice greatly, O daughter of Zion; shout O daughter of Jerusalem:

Schols. Behold thy King cometh unto thee: he is just and having salvation. Zech. ix. 9.

Sup. Behold a virgin shall bear a son and shall call his name Immanuel. Isa. vii. 14.

Schols. The angel said unto her, Fea·

not, Mary ; behold thou shalt bring forth
a son and shalt call his name JESUS.
Luke i. 30, 31.

Sup. Hosanna to the Son of David !
Blessed is he that cometh in the name of
the Lord !

Schols. Hosanna in the highest ! Matt.
xxi. 9.

Sup. This same Jesus which is taken up
from you into heaven, shall so come in
like manner as ye have seen him go into
heaven. Acts i. 11.

Schols. For the Lord himself shall descend from heaven with a shout, with the
voice of the archangel, and with the trump
of God. 1 Thess. iv. 16.

Sup. Behold I come quickly; and my
reward is with me, to give every man
according as his work shall be. Rev.
xxii. 12.

Schols. Let us therefore cast off the
works of darkness, and let us put on the
armour of light. Rom. xiii. 12.

Sup. The kingdoms of this world are become the kingdoms of our Lord and of his Christ;

Schols. And he shall reign for ever and ever.   Rev. xi. 15.

¶ *Here, and at the end of every Selection, may be said or sung the Gloria Patri.*

CHRISTMAS.

Sup. Behold, I bring you good tidings of great joy, which shall be to all people.

Schols. Unto you is born this day in the city of David, a Saviour which is Christ the Lord.   Luke ii. 10, 11.

Sup. Unto us a child is born, unto us a son is given : and his name shall be called—

Schols. Wonderful, Counsellor, the Mighty God, the Everlasting Father, the Prince of Peace.   Isa. ix. 6.

Sup. In the beginning was the Word, and the Word was with God, and the Word was God.

Schols. And the Word was made flesh, and dwelt among us.

Sup. And we beheld his glory, the glory as of the only begotten of the Father,

Schols. Full of grace and truth. John i. 1, 14.

Sup. For God so loved the world that he gave his only-begotten Son,

Schols. That whosoever believeth in him should not perish, but have everlasting life. John iii. 16.

Sup. Glory to God in the highest,

Schols. And on earth peace, good-will towards men. Luke ii. 14.

THE EPIPHANY.

Sup. Arise, shine; for thy light is come and the glory of the Lord is risen upon thee. Isa. lx. 1.

Schols. I am the light of the world; he that followeth me shall not walk in darkness, but shall have the light of life. John viii. 12.

Sup. The day-spring from on high hath visited us, to give light to them that sit in darkness and the shadow of death,

Schols. To guide our feet into the way of peace. Luke i. 78, 79.

Sup. God was manifest in the flesh,

Schols. Justified in the Spirit,

Sup. Seen of angels,

Schols. Preached unto the Gentiles,

Sup. Believed on in the world,

Schols. Received up into glory. 1 Tim. iii. 16.

Sup. The grace of God that bringeth salvation hath appeared to all men,

Schols. Teaching us that denying un-godliness and worldly lusts we should live—

Sup. Soberly, righteously, and godly in this present world;

Schols. Looking for that blessed hope, and the glorious appearing of the great

God and our Saviour Jesus Christ. Titus ii. 11, 13.

Sup. For the earth shall be full of the knowledge of the Lord,

Schols. As the waters cover the sea. Isa. xi. 9.

LENT.

Sup. Then was Jesus led up of the Spirit into the wilderness, to be tempted of the devil. Mat. iv. 1.

Schols. And he was there in the wilderness forty days, tempted of Satan; and the angels ministered unto him. Mark i. 13.

Sup. Blessed is the man that endureth temptation: for when he is tried—

Schols. He shall receive the crown of life, which the Lord hath promised to them that love him. James i. 12.

Sup. Repent and turn yourselves from all your transgressions, saith the Lord

God, so iniquity shall not be your ruin. Eze. xviii. 30.

Schols. Turn thou me, and I shall be turned; for thou art the Lord my God. Jer. xxxi. 18.

Sup. If we confess our sins, he is faithful and just to forgive us our sins, and to cleanse us from all unrighteousness. 1 John i. 9.

Schols. Father I have sinned against heaven and before thee, and am not worthy to be called thy son. Luke xv. 18.

Sup. Create in me a clean heart, O God,

Schols. And renew a right spirit within me. Ps. li. 10.

Sup. Search me, O God, and know my heart: try me, and know my thoughts:

Schols. And see if there be any wicked way in me, and lead me in the way everlasting. Ps. cxxxix. 23, 24.

PASSION WEEK.

Sup. Sacrifice and offering thou didst not desire ;

Schols. Burnt-offering and sin-offering hast thou not required.

Sup. Then said I, Lo, I come : in the volume of the book it is written of me,

Schols. I delight to do thy will, O my God.   Yea, thy law is within my heart. Ps. xl. 6-8.

Sup. And when they were come to the place called Calvary,

Schols. There they crucified him and the malefactors.

Sup. And the sun was darkened,

Schols. And the vail of the temple was rent in the midst.   Luke xxiii. 33, 45.

Sup. He said, " It is finished ; "

Schols. And he bowed his head and gave up the ghost.   John xix. 30.

Sup. Surely he hath borne our griefs and carried our sorrows :

Schols. He was wounded for our transgressions, he was bruised for our iniquities.

Sup. He is brought as a lamb to the slaughter. Isa. liii. 4, 5, 7.

Schols. Behold the Lamb of God which taketh away the sin of the world! John i. 29.

Sup. Let this mind be in you which was also in Christ Jesus. ·

Schols. He humbled himself and became obedient unto death, even the death of the cross. Philip. ii. 5.

Sup. Worthy is the Lamb that was slain to receive power and riches, and strength and honour, and glory and blessing;

Schols. For thou wast slain, and hast redeemed us to God by thy blood. Rev. v. 12, 9.

EASTER.

Sup. The Lord is risen indeed. Luke xxiv. 34.

Schols. Blessed are they that have not seen, and yet have believed. John xx. 29.

Sup. Blessed be the God and Father of our Lord Jesus Christ, who according to his abundant mercy

Schols. Hath begotten us again unto a lively hope, by the resurrection of Jesus Christ from the dead.   1 Pet. i. 3.

Sup. And very early in the morning, the first day of the week,

Schols. They came unto the sepulchre at the rising of the sun.   Mark xvi. 2.

Sup. And they found the stone rolled away from the sepulchre.

Schols. And they entered in, and found not the body of the Lord Jesus.

Sup. And behold, two men stood by them in shining garments:

Schols. And they said, Why seek ye the living among the dead?

Sup. He is not here, but is risen:

Schols. And they remembered his words. Luke xxiv. 2, 3, 4, 5, 6, 8.

Sup. I am the resurrection and the life :
Schols. He that believeth in me, though he were dead yet shall he live. John xi. 25.

Sup. Now is Christ risen from the dead,
Schols. And become the first-fruits of them that slept.

Sup. Thanks be to God, which giveth us the victory—
Schols. Through our Lord Jesus Christ. 1 Cor. xv. 20, 57.

ASCENSION.

Sup. What and if ye shall see the Son of man ascend up where he was before? John vi. 62.

Schols. I ascend unto my Father, and your Father; and to my God, and your God. John xx. 17.

Sup. And he led them out as far as to Bethany, and he lifted up his hands and blessed them.

Schols. And while he blessed them he

was parted from them and carried up into heaven.   Luke xxiv. 50, 51.

Sup. Who is gone into heaven, and is on the right hand of God;

Schols. Angels and authorities and powers being made subject unto him.   1 Peter. iii. 21.

Sup. I go to prepare a place for you.

Schols. And if I go, I will come again and receive you unto myself. John xiv. 2, 3.

Sup. Lift up your heads, O ye gates; and be ye lift up, ye everlasting doors;

Schols. And the King of glory shall come in.

Sup. Who is this King of glory?

Schols. The Lord of hosts, he is the King of glory.   Ps. xxiv. 7, 10.

Sup. To him be glory and dominion—

Schols. For ever and ever. Amen. Rev. i. 6.

WHIT-SUNDAY.

Sup. It shall come to pass that I will pour out my Spirit upon all flesh ;

Schols. And your sons and your daughters shall prophesy.   Joel ii. 28.

Sup. I will put my Spirit within you,

Schols. And cause you to walk in my tatutes.   Eze. xxxvi. 27.

Sup. When the Comforter is come, whom will send unto you from the Father,

Schols. Even the Spirit of truth, which proceedeth from the Father ;—John xv. 26.

Sup. He shall teach you all things,

Schols. And bring all things to your remembrance whatsoever I have said unto you.   John xiv. 26.

Sup. Ye shall receive power—

Schols. After that the Holy Ghost is come upon you.   Acts i. 8.

Sup. And when the day of Pentecost

was fully come, they were all with one accord in one place.

Schols. And suddenly there came a sound from heaven as of a mighty rushing wind;

Sup. And there appeared unto them cloven tongues like as of fire;

Schols. And it sat upon each of them.

Sup. And they were all filled with the Holy Ghost;

Schols. And began to speak with other tongues, as the Spirit gave them utterance.   Acts ii. 1, 2, 3, 4.

Sup. Hereby know we that we dwell in him, and he in us,

Schols. Because he hath given us of his Spirit.   1 John iv. 13.

Sup. As many as are led by the Spirit of God they are the sons of God.   Rom. viii. 14.

Schols. The fruit of the Spirit is love, joy, peace, long-suffering, gentleness, goodness, faith.   Gal. v. 22, 23.

TRINITY.

Sup. Hear O Israel! the Lord our God is one Lord.   Deut. vi. 4.

Schols. One God and Father of all, who is above all, and through all and in you all.   Eph. iv. 6.

Sup. I and my Father are one.   John x. 30.

Schols. In the beginning was the Word, and the Word was with God, and the Word was God.   John i. 1.

Sup. The Comforter, which is the Holy Ghost: John xiv. 26.

Schols. Even the Spirit of truth which proceedeth from the Father.   John xv. 26.

Sup. Go ye therefore, and teach all nations,

Schols. Baptizing them in the name of the Father, and of the Son, and of the Holy Ghost.   Mat. xxviii. 19.

Sup. The Father, of Whom are all things,

Schols. And we in Him;

Sup. Jesus Christ, by Whom are all things,

Schols. And we by Him:

Sup. The Holy Ghost, Who dwelleth with you,

Schols. And shall be in you.

Sup. Holy, holy, holy, Lord God Almighty.

Schols. Which was, and is, and is to come.   Rev. iv. 8.

Sup. The grace of our Lord Jesus Christ and the love of God, and the fellowship of the Holy Ghost be with you all.

Schols. Amen.   2 Cor. xiii. 14.

Glory be to the Father, and to the Son, and to the Holy Ghost;

As it was in the beginning, is now and ever shall be, world without end.   Amen.

OFFICES OF DEVOTION.

MORNING EXERCISE.

RESPONSIVE SELECTION. *Wisdom's counsel.*

Superintendent. My son, forget not my law: but let thine heart keep my commandments. Prov. iii. 1.

Scholars. For length of days, and long life, and peace, shall they add to thee. 2.

Superintendent. Let not mercy and truth forsake thee: bind them about thy neck, write them upon the table of thine heart. 3.

Scholars. So shalt thou find favor and good understanding in the sight of God and man. 4.

Superintendent. Trust in the Lord with

all thine heart, and lean not to thine own understanding. 5.

Scholars. In all thy ways acknowledge him, and he shall direct thy paths. 6.

Superintendent. Happy is the man that findeth wisdom, and the man that getteth understanding. 13.

Scholars. For the merchandise of it is better than the merchandise of silver, and the gain thereof, than fine gold. 14.

Superintendent. She is more precious than rubies; and all the things thou canst desire are not to be compared unto her. 15.

Scholars. Length of days is in her right hand, and in her left hand riches and honor. 16.

Superintendent. Her ways are ways of pleasantness, and all her paths are peace. 17.

Scholars. She is a tree of life to them that lay hold upon her; and happy is every one that retaineth her. 18.

Superintendent. Let us pray. [COLLECT.]

Almighty God, our Heavenly Father, we praise and bless thy holy name for thy preservation of us during another week, and for permitting us to meet together in our school on the morning of this holy day. (Special praise.)*

We beseech thee to hear us, good Lord.

We appear before thee, O Lord, as sinful creatures. Make us deeply sensible of our sins, and blot them out from thy sight, for Jesus Christ's sake.

We beseech thee to hear us, good Lord.

We pray thee to meet with us, O Lord, and grant us thine aid, in the important work in which we are now to be engaged. Look graciously, we beseech thee, upon the members of this school. Make the teachers sensible of the great charge committed to their trust. Endue them plenteously with heavenly gifts, and dispose them to labor with faithfulness and zeal, in train-

* The italicized responses are for teachers and children

ing these scholars in thy fear and service.

We beseech thee to hear us, good Lord.

And be thou with these scholars, O Lord, in love and mercy. May they from the heart believe in thee, their Creator, Redeemer and Sanctifier. Grant that the instructions which they here receive may be truly believed and truly followed, all the days of their life. May they trust in the Lord with all their hearts, and not lean to their own understanding. In all their ways may they acknowledge thee, and do thou direct their paths.

We beseech thee to hear us, good Lord.

Graft in the hearts of our scholars the love of thy name, increase in them true religion, nourish them with all goodness, and of thy great mercy keep them in the same, that so having served thee faithfully in this world, they may obtain everlasting life, through the merits of Jesus Christ our Saviour, to whom, with the Father and the

Holy Ghost, be all power and glory, world without end.   Amen.

Our Father, who art in heaven, hallow-ed be thy name; thy kingdom come; thy will be done, on earth as it is in heaven. Give us this day our daily bread : forgive us our trespasses, as we forgive those who trespass against us : and lead us not into temptation, but deliver us from evil : for thine is the kingdom, and the power, and the glory for ever and ever.   Amen.

The grace of our Lord Jesus Christ, and the love of God, and the fellowship of the Holy Ghost, be with us all evermore. Amen.

RESPONSIVE SELECTIONS. *The invitations of the Gospel.*

Superintendent. Ho, every one that thirsteth, come ye to the waters, and he that hath no money, come ye, buy and eat.

Scholars. Yea, come, buy wine and milk, without money and without price. Isaiah lv. 1.

Superintendent. Incline your ear and come unto me; hear, and your soul shall live.

Scholars. And I will make an everlasting covenant with you, even the sure mercies of David. 3.

Superintendent. The Spirit and the Bride say, Come, and let him that heareth say, Come.

Scholars. Let him that is athirst, come:

(24)

and whosoever will, let him take the water of life freely.   Rev. xxii. 17.

Superintendent.   Come unto me all ye that labor and are heavy laden, and I will give you rest.   Matt. xi. 28.

Scholars.   Take my yoke upon you and learn of me; for I am meek and lowly in heart, and ye shall find rest unto your souls.   29.

Superintendent.   All that the Father giveth me shall come to me.

Scholars.   And him that cometh to me I will in no wise cast out.   John vi. 37.

Superintendent.   Jesus said, Whosoever drinketh of this water shall thirst again: but whosoever drinketh of the water that I shall give him, shall never thirst.

Scholars.   But the water that I shall give him shall be in him a well of water springing up into everlasting life.   John iv. 13, 14.

Superintendent.   Look unto me all ye ends of the earth, and be ye saved; for beside me there is no Saviour Isaiah xiv. 22.

Scholars. Him hath God exalted with his right hand to be a Prince and a Saviour, to give repentance to Israel and forgiveness of sins. Acts v. 31.

Superintendent. Let us pray. [Collect.]

Our heavenly Father, we desire to give thanks unto thee, and to praise thy name: to show forth thy loving-kindness in the morning, and thy faithfulness every night. Every day would we bless thee, and praise thy name for ever and ever. For thou art gracious, O Lord, and full of compassion: slow to anger and of great mercy. Thou art good to all, and thy tender mercies are over all thy works. Thou art nigh unto them that call upon thee. O, may we feel thee near to us: be near to us, now while we are seeking to draw near to thee; be near us when we read thy word, and listen to its teachings, and in all that we attempt to do this day.

Lord, let our cry come before thee.

We thank thee, our Father, that we are brought in safety to the beginning of another Sabbath. Bless us, we pray thee, in all its privileges and duties. We thank thee that we live in a land of Sabbaths and sanctuaries—of Bibles and Sunday-schools; O, make us to feel how much we are favored in having these blessings; and how solemn an account we shall have to give of them at last. May we all strive to improve our privileges this day, as we should desire to do if we knew it was to be our last Sabbath on earth.

Lord, let our cry come before thee.

Bless, O Lord, we pray thee, all the teachers of this school. Unite our hearts together in Christian love and confidence. May we all be of one mind in prosecuting our important work. Give us wisdom, and zeal, and love, and patience and perseverance, and everything necessary for the faithful discharge of our duties. And, O, crown our feeble labors, Lord, we pray thee, with abundant success.

Lord, let our cry come before thee.

Bless all our dear scholars here before thee. Teach them to remember their Creator in the days of their youth. Guide their feet into the way of peace. Open their hearts to receive thy truth. Make them sensible of their great sinfulness, and work in them true repentance for all their transgressions. May they feel their need of the renewing influence of the Holy Spirit, and be led to seek that change of heart and holiness of life, without which they cannot enter the kingdom of heaven.

Lord, let our cry come before thee.

O bless the instruction that may be communicated to our scholars this day: may it sink deep into their hearts, like seed in good ground: may it be quickened there by the power of the Holy Spirit: and spring up, and grow, and bear fruit a hundred fold to the glory of thy name.

Lord, let our cry come before thee.

Bless the other schools connected with our Church. Bless all the Sunday-schools in our land, and in the world: may the children instructed in them grow up in thy fear, and live to thy glory. Bless the schools that have been established in heathen lands: and let the dark places of the earth, that are filled with the habitations of cruelty, soon be enlightened and cheered with the glorious gospel of thy dear Son. Hear us, O Lord, in these our prayers, pardon all our sins, and accept us, now and ever, for Jesus' sake. Amen.

Our Father, etc.

The grace of our Lord, etc.

Third Sunday Morning.

RESPONSIVE SELECTION.   *The way of salvation.*

Superintendent.   Jesus saith, I am the way, the truth, and the life; no man cometh unto the Father but by me.   John xiv. 6.

Scholars.   The law was given by Moses, but grace and truth came by Jesus Christ. John i. 17.

Superintendent.   Jesus said, Verily, verily I say unto you, I am the door of the sheep; by me if any man enter in, he shall be saved, and shall go in and out and find pasture.   John x. 7–9.

Scholars.   This is the stone which was set at nought by the builders, which is become the head of the corner, neither is there salvation in any other, for there is none other name under heaven given

among men, whereby we must be saved
Acts iv. 11, 12.

Superintendent. Jesus answered, Verily,
verily I say unto you, Except a man be
born again, he cannot see the kingdom of
God.   John iii. 3.

Scholars. And Jesus called a little child
unto him, and said, Verily I say unto you,
Except ye be converted, and become as
little children, ye shall not enter into the
kingdom of heaven.   Matt. xviii. 2, 3.

Superintendent. God so loved the world,
that he gave his only begotten Son, that
whosoever believeth in Him should not
perish, but have everlasting life.   John iii.
16.

Scholars. To him give all the prophets
witness, that, through his name, whosoever
believeth in him, shall receive remission
of sins.   Acts x. 43.

Superintendent. Thou hast given him
power over all flesh, that he should give
eternal life to as many as thou hast given

him; and this is life eternal, that they might know thee, the only true God, and Jesus Christ whom thou hast sent. John xvii. 2, 3.

Scholars. Wherefore he is able to save unto the uttermost, all that come unto God by him, seeing he ever liveth to make intercession for them. Hebrews vii. 25.

Superintendent. This is the record, that God hath given to us eternal life, and this life is in his Son. 1 John v. 11.

Scholars. He that believeth on the Son, hath everlasting life; but he that believeth not the Son, shall not see life, but the wrath of God abideth on him. John iii. 36.

Superintendent. Let us pray. [Collect.]

Let the words of our mouths, and the meditations of our hearts, be always acceptable in thy sight, O Lord, our strength, and our Redeemer!

[We praise thee, O Lord, we call upon our souls, and all that is within us, to bless thy holy name. Thou forgivest all our iniquities; thou healest all our infirmities thou savest our life from destruction; thou crownest us with loving-kindness and tender mercies. For thou art merciful, O Lord, and gracious, slow to anger, and plenteous in goodness and in truth. Thou hast not dealt with us after our sins, nor rewarded us according to our iniquities. Like as a father pitieth his children, so thou, O Lord, dost pity them that fear thee. For thou knowest our frame; thou rememberest that we are but dust.]*

We praise thee, O Lord, for the return of another Sabbath, and we pray thee, with the light of this blessed morning, to lift upon us the light of thy reconciled countenance. Bless us, we beseech Thee, our Father, in all the duties and privileges of this day. Help us to make a right improve-

* The clauses in brackets may be omitted at the discretion of the Superintendent.

ment of the precious means of grace now afforded us.

Hear us, O Lord, for Jesus' sake.

We have met together to read thy holy word, and try to learn its meaning; but we cannot do this without the help of thy Spirit. O, send down upon us, we pray thee, then, the blessed influences of the Holy Spirit, to enlighten our minds, that we may understand thy truth, and to open our hearts to receive it; and may it make us wise unto salvation, through faith in thee.

Hear us, O Lord, for Jesus' sake.

[Give us an increasing love for thy word; may it be a light to our feet, and a lamp to our path, in our pilgrimage through this benighted world. May we ever make it the man of our counsel, and our guide, and may it teach us to know thee, the only true God, and Jesus Christ whom thou hast sent.]

Bless all the teachers of our schools, O

Lord. Make us wise to win souls. May we know by experience the truths we attempt to teach. May the love of Christ constrain us, and the grace of Christ assist us in the performance of our duty. May we be earnest, and diligent, faithful, and persevering in our work; may we never faint or be weary in it, and in due time may we reap an abundant harvest.

Hear us, O Lord, for Jesus' sake.

Look graciously, O Heavenly Father, we pray thee, on all these dear scholars. Bless to them the instruction they may receive from thy word this day. May thy Holy Spirit cause them to understand its meaning, and feel its power. May they be led to see their lost and ruined condition by nature, and seek and secure an interest in Christ as their Saviour. May they repent truly of their sins, and exercise true faith in Jesus. May their hearts be changed by thy grace; may all evil tempers and dispositions be taken away from them; may they be kind and affectionate one to another; respectful and attentive to their teachers, and obedient and dutiful to their parents.

Hear us, O Lord, for Jesus' sake.

Keep them, O Lord, we beseech thee, from all the sins and temptations of this wicked world; may they grow up in the nurture and admonition of the Lord; may thy fear be before their eyes all their days; and may they so pass through things temporal, that, finally, they lose not the things eternal. Hear us, O Lord, in these our prayers, and accept us now and ever, through Jesus Christ our Saviour. Amen.

Our Father, etc.

The grace of our Lord, etc.

Fourth Sunday Morning.

Responsive Selection. *The happiness of the Christian.*

Superintendent. If any man be in Christ, he is a new creature; old things are passed away; behold all things are become new. 2 Cor. v. 17.

Scholars. There is, therefore, now no condemnation to them that are in Christ Jesus. Romans viii. 1.

Superintendent. Therefore, being justified by faith, we have peace with God through our Lord Jesus Christ. Romans v. 1.

Scholars. The peace of God, which passeth all understanding, shall keep our hearts and minds through Jesus Christ. Phil. iv. 7.

Superintendent. Blessed is he whose

transgression is forgiven, whose sin is covered.   Psalm xxxii. 1.

Scholars.   Surely he shall not be moved for ever; the righteous shall be had in everlasting remembrance.   Psalms cxii. 6.

Superintendent.   Say ye to the righteous, it shall be well with him.   Isa. iii. 10.

Scholars.   All the paths of the Lord are mercy and truth to such as keep his covenant and his testimonies.   Psalm xxv. 10.

Superintendent.   Blessed is the man whom thou choosest, and causest to approach unto thee, that he may dwell in thy courts.   Psalm lxv. 4.

Scholars.   He shall be satisfied with the goodness of thy house, even of thy holy temple.   Psalm lxv. 4.

Superintendent.   And who is he that shall harm you, if ye be followers of that which is good?   1 Pet. iii. 13.

Scholars. The Lord is my light and my salvation ; whom shall I fear? the Lord is the strength of my life; of whom shall I be afraid?   Psalm xxvii. 1.

Superintendent.   Happy are the people that are in such a case; yea, happy are the people whose God is the Lord.   Psalm cxliv. 15.

Scholars.   For the Lord God is a sun and a shield; the Lord will give grace and glory; and no good thing will he withhold from them that walk uprightly.   Psalm lxxxiv. 11.

Superintendent.   Let us pray.

Merciful and gracious God, our Heavenly Father, we bless thy holy name for thy preservation of us from the beginning of our lives to the present hour; and especially for thy care and protection of us through the dangers of the past week, and the darkness of the past night

Receive our praises, O Lord.   [COLLECT.]

We thank thee that, while many have been taken away by death, we are spared in life.   We thank thee that, while many are suffering from pain and sickness, we are blessed with health. We thank thee that, while many are deprived of the use of their reason, we are kept in our right minds, and are permitted to use them in studying thy Word, and in learning thy will.

O Lord, accept our prayers.

We thank thee that, while multitudes in other lands have no Bibles, and no Sabbaths, and no sanctuaries, we are favored with all these great blessings. And we thank thee that, at the beginning of this holy day, we are permitted to come up to this thine house, and engage again in the pleasant duties and delightful privileges which are now before us. Bless us, O heavenly Father, in all the engagements of this day.

O Lord, accept our prayers.

Look graciously, we pray thee, on all our teachers. Give them thy heavenly wisdom and thy rich grace. Teach them to understand thy holy word: and help them, by thy blessed Spirit, to make it

plain to their scholars. Fill their hearts
with love to thee, O blessed Saviour; and
help them, in proof of that love, faithfully
and diligently to feed thy lambs.

O Lord, accept our prayers.

Look down in mercy on all these dear
scholars. Bless to them the instruction
that may be given this day. Open their
eyes to see, their ears to hear, and their
hearts to understand thy truth. O, make
them wise unto salvation. Teach them
truly to repent of their sins, and to believe
with all their hearts in Jesus, as their Saviour. May they all be made thy children, and partakers of the blessings of thy
salvation.

O Lord, accept our prayers.

Bless their parents and friends, and all
connected with them. Look graciously on
our church and all who worship here.
Bless thy word as it is preached in this
place, and make it the power of God unto
salvation to all who hear it.

O Lord, accept our prayers.

Bless thy word wherever it is made known to-day, either by ministers or teachers; both in our own land, and in all other places. And hasten, we pray thee, O Lord, the coming of that time when all shall know thee, from the least unto the greatest; and the earth shall be filled with the knowledge of the Lord, as the waters cover the sea.

O Lord, accept our prayers.

These mercies, and whatever else thou shalt see to be necessary and convenient for us, we humbly beg, in the name and mediation of thy Son our Saviour, Jesus Christ, who taught us when we pray to say —Our Father, etc.

The grace of our Lord, etc.

RESPONSIVE SELECTION. *Encouragements to prayer.*

Superintendent. Ask, and it shall be given you; seek, and ye shall find; knock, and it shall be opened unto you. Matt. vii. 7.

Scholars. For every one that asketh receiveth; and he that seeketh findeth; and to him that knocketh, it shall be opened. Matt. vii. 8.

Superintendent. The Lord is nigh unto all them that call upon him, to all that call on him in truth. Psalm clxv. 18.

Scholars. He will fulfil the desire of them that fear him; he will also hear their cry, and will save them. Psalm cxlv. 19.

Superintendent. All things whatsoever

ye shall ask in prayer, believing, ye shall receive.   Matt. xxi. 22.

Scholars.   Ask, and ye shall receive, that your joy may be full.   John xvi. 24.

Superintendent.   What profit should we have, if we pray unto him.   Job xxi. 15.

Scholars.   He shall call upon me, and I will answer him; I will be with him in trouble; I will deliver him and honor him.   Psalm xci. 15.

Superintendent.   Call upon me in the day of trouble, I will deliver thee, and thou shalt glorify me.   Psalm l. 15.

Scholars.   The righteous cry, and the Lord heareth, and delivereth them out of all their troubles.   Psalm xxxiv. 15.

Superintendent.   The Lord is rich in mercy to all that call on him.   Romans v. 8.

Scholars.   If two of you shall agree on earth, as touching anything that they shall ask, it shall be done for them, of my Father which is in heaven.   Matt. xviii. 19.

Superintendent. Whosoever shall call on the name of the Lord shall be saved. Joel ii. 32.

Scholars. For there is no difference between the Jew and the Greek, for the same Lord over all, is rich unto all who call upon him. Rom. x. 12.

Superintendent. Let us pray. [Collect.]

Almighty God, our Heavenly Father, we thank thee that we are permitted to meet together on this holy Sabbath. We would unite to worship thee in spirit and in truth.

[We praise thee as our Divine Creator in whom we live, and move, and have our being. We bless thee as our Gracious Redeemer, who hast borne our sins on the cross, and died, and risen again for us, that we might have eternal life in thee. We adore thee as our Heavenly Comforter and Sanctifier, by whose power alone we can become new creatures, and live to the glory of God. In thine hand, O Lord, our breath is, and thine are all our ways]

Receive our praises, O Lord.

We praise thee this morning, our Heavenly Father, for all the blessings and privileges which we enjoy. Great and manifold have been thy mercies to us. We bless thee for the opportunity now afforded us of meeting in thy house, to hear and study thy holy word, and to make known our wants to thee in prayer.

Receive our praises, O Lord.

Wilt thou graciously meet with us this day, and teach and guide us all by thy Holy Spirit? May we learn more of thee, that we may love thee better, and more of ourselves, that we may be truly sorry for our sins, and seek thy pardon of them.

Lord, hear our prayers.

We would come before thee, O, our Father, with the deepest humility. We acknowledge our past neglect of thy mercies to us, and our failure to improve them. We have been too unthankful for thy blessed Gospel, and too heedless of the blessed influences of thy Holy Spirit. We pray thee to forgive us all that is past, for Jesus' sake.

Lord, hear our prayers.

Our Heavenly Father, we beseech thee to bless all our dear relatives and friends with heavenly blessings in Christ Jesus. Comfort and support them in all their sorrows and troubles, with the consolations of thy Blessed Spirit. May our earthly parents, and our brothers and sisters, always be the children of our Heavenly Father.

Lord, hear our prayers.

May our pastor, whom thou hast set over us in thy house, be a faithful shepherd and guide to us, and may we be able to profit and improve much by his instructions. Let all thy ministers be strengthened by thy heavenly grace, and let the knowledge of thy Gospel be spread through all nations. Have pity on the multitudes who are destitute of the privileges we enjoy.

Lord, hear our prayers.

Be merciful to the heathen, who know thee not, and the people who call not on thy name, that they may hear thy truth, and turn to thee and live. Graciously hear our prayers, accept our praises, and bless us in all our works, begun, continued, and ended in thee, for the sake of Jesus Christ our Saviour, in whose words we conclude our prayers.

Lord, hear our prayers.

Our Father, etc.

The grace of our Lord, etc.

AFTERNOON PRAYERS.

The Morning Service can be used, with verbal changes when the afternoon is the only session.

No. I.

[COLLECT.]

Oh, merciful and gracious God! Thou art the Author and Source of every blessing, and our praise belongeth always unto thee We thank thee that we have enjoyed the privileges of thy blessed Gospel through another holy Sabbath day.

We praise thee, O God.

Enable us to embrace the blessed invitations of our Saviour to come unto him, and to walk in his steps. Take away from us every sinful and unholy temper, and make us gentle unto all men. May we have that meek and lowly mind which was in our blessed Redeemer, and learn to do unto all as we would have them do unto us.

We beseech thee to hear us, O Lord.

May we humbly obey our parents, and try in every way to promote their comfort and happiness. May we be kind and affectionate to our brothers and sisters, and lay aside all malice and wrath, and evil speaking. May we everywhere maintain the spirit of peace and love, and follow the example our blessed Lord in all things.

We beseech thee to hear us, O Lord.

And grant, O Lord, that we may have a

heart to love and praise thee; seeking thy favor and forgiveness in daily prayer; delighting in the study of thy Holy Word; and endeavouring to walk more humbly with thee our God. Give us that holiness, without which no man shall see the Lord; and enable us to grow in grace, and in the knowledge of our Lord and Saviour Jesus Christ.

We beseech thee to hear us, O Lord.

O, may we seek thee early, and seek thee always, that we may find thee as our portion forever, and be rendered meet to be partakers of the inheritance of the saints in light. And when all our precious opportunities of religious instruction and worship are finished, may we be received into thy eternal and heavenly kingdom, through Christ, our blessed Lord, in whose words we sum up our imperfect prayers.

Our Father, etc.

The grace of our Lord, etc.

No. II.
[COLLECT.]

Almighty God, who art always more ready to hear than we to pray, and art wont to give more than we either desire, or deserve, give ear unto our voice, when we call upon thee. Let our prayer be set forth before thee as incense, and the lifting up of our hands as an evening sacrifice.

Hear us, O Lord, for Jesus' sake.

[Show us thy marvellous loving-kindness, O thou that savest by thy right hand, those who put their trust in thee! Keep us as the apple of thine eye; hide us under the shadow of thy wing; for thou, Lord, only makest us to dwell in safety. O, satisfy us early with thy mercy, that we may rejoice and be glad all our days.

Hear us, O Lord, for Jesus' sake.]

How excellent is thy loving-kindness, O God! therefore may we put our trust under the shadow of thy wings. May we be abundantly satisfied with the fulness of thy house, and do thou make us drink of the river of thy pleasures. For with thee is the fountain of life, and in thy light may we see light. Be thou our Shepherd, O Lord! that we may not want. Make us to lie down in green pastures; lead us beside the still waters. O, convert our souls, and lead us in the paths of righteousness, for thy name's sake.

Hear us, O Lord, for Jesus' sake.

Teach us, O Lord, the way of thy statutes, that we may keep it unto the end. Give us understanding, that we may keep thy law, yea, that we may observe it with our whole hearts. Turn away our eyes from beholding vanity, and quicken us in thy way. May thy word be hid in our hearts, that we may not sin against thee.

Hear us, O Lord, for Jesus' sake.

May we rejoice in the way of thy testimonies, more than in all riches. May we meditate in thy precepts, and have respect unto thy ways. Open thou our eyes that we may behold wonderful things out of thy law; and let thy testimonies be our delight and our counsellor.

Hear us, O Lord, for Jesus' sake.

Receive our humble thanksgiving, O Lord, for all the mercies and blessings of this Sabbath day. Pardon all our short-comings and offences, and the sin that mingles with our holiest services. Be with us during the remainder of this holy day, and bless it abundantly to our souls. Be with us through all this week, and keep us from sin and danger, and from every evil.

Hear us, O Lord, for Jesus' sake.

Give ear, O Lord, unto our prayer, and hide not thyself from our supplications. Let thy work appear unto thy servants, and thy glory unto our children. And let the beauty of the Lord our God be upon us; and establish thou the work of our hands; yea, the work of our hands, establish thou it, for the sake of thy Son, our Saviour, Jesus Christ. Amen.

No. III.

[COLLECT.]

O Lord, thou art the high and holy One who inhabitest eternity! Thou art the great and glorious God, and we are poor sinful creatures. We are not worthy to come near thy throne or to ask any favor at thy hands. The angels bow down with reverence in thy presence, and veil their faces before thee. May we all feel when we come into thy presence, that thine eye is looking directly at each one of us, and may we never be thoughtless or trifling in our prayers.

We beseech thee to hear us, good Lord.

Look upon us in mercy, in these our opening exercises, this afternoon. We thank thee for the blessings and privileges we have enjoyed this day, and for those now before us. We bless thee for all the means of grace, and for the hope of glory.

We beseech thee to hear us, good Lord.

Be present with us in our school at this

time. Give grace to our teachers, to be patient, and diligent, and persevering. May they never faint or be weary, but always abound in the work of the Lord, knowing that their labor is not in vain in the Lord. And while we plant and water, help us to look in faith to thee for the increase. And, O Lord, grant to us that heavenly increase for which we pray.

We beseech thee to hear us, good Lord.

Come into our school in all the power of thy conquering grace. Lead these dear scholars to repent and turn to thee with all their hearts. May they, with Mary, make choice of that good part which shall never be taken away from them.

We beseech thee to hear us, good Lord.

O, call us, as thou didst call Samuel, while we are young; and teach us to hear thy voice; and like him, may each one of us say, "Speak, Lord, for thy servant heareth." O, let us not grow up in hardness of heart, and contempt of thy word and commandment, but satisfy us early with thy mercy, that we may rejoice and be glad all the days of our life.

We beseech thee to hear us, good Lord.

May the instructions of this day sink deep in their hearts, like seed sown in good ground, and bring forth fruit an hundred fold.

We beseech thee to hear us, good Lord.

Pardon all our sins. Help us to keep the Sabbath day holy unto the end of it. And when our earthly Sabbaths are over, may we all meet in thy presence above, and spend an eternal Sabbath amidst the glory and blessedness of thine everlasting kingdom, through Jesus Christ our Lord. Amen.

No. IV.
[COLLECT.]

O Lord, our heavenly Father, we beseech thee to accept the offering of our praise, and to visit us with thy salvation.

How great has been thy goodness to us through all our life! If we would count thy mercies, they are more than we can number. Blessed be thy name, for all thy benefits. We are unworthy, sinful creatures: O, teach us to be truly grateful for all thy love. To thy great mercy we owe it that we are still alive, and have not been cut off in the midst of our sins.

Lord, let our cry come before thee.

Our Heavenly Father, we cannot praise thee, or pray to thee as we ought, without thy help. O, let thy Holy Spirit help our infirmities, and teach us how to pray. May we enjoy thy presence through the remainder of this day, and be able to keep thy Sabbath holy unto the end of it. Give us humble hearts to hear and to read thy word. Assist and direct our pastor and our teachers, in their efforts to instruct us in thy truths. Create and make in us new and contrite hearts, that we may truly re-

pent of all our sins, and obtain thy par
doning mercy.

Lord, let our cry come before thee.

Lord, thou hast cast our life in pleasant places. We have a goodly heritage. Thou hast blest us with great and precious blessings. We would thank thee for them all. We thank thee for our connection with this school, and for all the pleasant hours we have spent here together.

Lord, let our cry come before thee.

We thank thee for thy holy Church, and for the permission to unite in its worship, and to receive thy instructions through its ministry. O, bless all these appointed means for our salvation, by the teaching and power of thy Holy Spirit. May we be guided and sanctified by his grace.

Lord, let our cry come before thee.

Bless our school with spiritual prosperity and success. Bless our teachers with wisdom, and patience, and love, to be thy messengers of good to us. Bless our parents and friends with a knowledge and enjoyment of thy truth and favor. Make us a blessing to them, and to all with whom we are connected in life.

Lord, let our cry come before thee.

Bear with our infirmities; pardon all our sins; and receive us into thy heavenly family as the children of God for ever, through the merits and death of our blessed Lord and Saviour, Jesus Christ.—Amen.

Our Father, etc.

The grace of our Lord, etc.

CLOSING PRAYERS.

Dismiss us with thy blessing, we pray, O Lord, now, as we depart from our school. Help us to remember the truth we have now learned from thy Holy Word. May it sink deep into our hearts, like seed sown in good ground. May it be watered there by the dew of thy grace. May it be quickened by the power of thy Spirit, and bring forth fruit abundantly in the hearts and lives of these dear scholars, to the honor and praise of thy holy name. Teach them all to know, and love, and serve thee. Guide them by thy counsel through this wilderness, and afterwards receive them to glory.

Lord, let our cry come before thee.

Go with us, O Lord, now, when we are about to enter thine earthly temple. May we feel thy presence there. Teach us to reverence thy sanctuary. Keep us from all foolish thoughts, or trifling words or conduct. Help us to worship thee acceptably, in spirit and in truth.

O Lord, hear us for Jesus' sake.

Bless to our souls, the exercises in which we may engage; or the truths we may hear while before thee there. And give us grace so to improve all the privileges we now enjoy, that at last we may come to thine heavenly kingdom, through Jesus Christ our Lord.   Amen.

No. II.

At the close of our school, we look to thee, O, our Heavenly Father, for thy blessing to rest upon the instruction which has now been given. Without thy blessing nothing can prosper. Paul may plant, and Apollos water, but thou alone canst give the increase.

Lord, hear us in our prayers.

We desire to commit ourselves to thy gracious care and keeping. We need a guide : we need a keeper. O, take us, we beseech thee, under thy Fatherly care and protection.   Hold us in the hollow of thy hand. Keep us as the apple of thine eye.   Preserve us from all the snares, and temptations, and sins, that are in the world. Help us to make thy blessed Word the guide of our life. Help us to carry out into daily practice the lessons we are here taught.

Lord, hear us in our prayers.

When we go up to thy sanctuary, may we remember that "Thou, God, seest us." When we go to our homes, may we show, by obedience to those who are over us, and by kindness and tenderness to all around us, that we are really made better by the study of thy Word. May we tread in the blessed steps of thy most holy life, O Lord, our Saviour! Like thee, may we increase in wisdom and stature, and in favor with God and man. And at last may we all be brought to thine heavenly kingdom, and we will give all the praise to the Father, the Son, and the Holy Spirit, world without end. Amen.

The grace of our Lord, etc.

II.

———

THE

Order of Evening Prayer,

WITH

SPECIAL CANTICLES,

ARRANGED FOR

THE CHILDREN'S CHURCH SERVICE.

EVENING PRAYER.

¶ *The Minister shall begin the* EVENING PRAYER, *by read-ing one or more of the following Sentences of Scripture.*

THE LORD is in his holy temple ; let all the earth keep silence before him. *Hab.* ii. 20.

Let the words of my mouth, and the meditation of my heart, be alway accept-able in thy sight, O Lord, my strength and my redeemer. *Psalm* xix. 14, 15.

I will arise, and go to my father, and will say unto him, Father, I have sinned against heaven, and before thee, and am no more worthy to be called thy son. *St. Luke* xv. 18, 19.

If we say that we have no sin, we de-ceive ourselves, and the truth is not in us ; but if we confess our sins, God is faithful and just to forgive us our sins, and to cleanse us from all unrighteousness.   1 *John* i. 8, 9.

¶ *Then the Minister shall say,*

DEARLY beloved, the Scripture moveth us, in sundry places, to acknowledge and confess our manifold sins and wickedness; and that we should not dissemble nor cloak them before the face of Almighty God, our heavenly Father; but confess them with an humble, lowly, penitent, and obedient heart; to the end that we may obtain forgiveness of the same, by his infinite goodness and mercy. And although we ought, at all times, humbly to acknowledge our sins before God; yet ought we chiefly so to do, when we assemble and meet together to render thanks for the great benefits that we have received at his hands, to set forth his most. worthy praise, to hear his most holy Word, and to ask those things which are requisite and necessary, as well for the body as the soul. Wherefore I pray and beseech you, as many as are here present, to accompany me with a pure heart, and humble voice, unto the throne of the heavenly grace, saying—

A General Confession.

¶ *To be said by the whole Congregation, after the Minister, all kneeling.*

ALMIGHTY and most merciful Father; We have erred and strayed from thy ways like lost sheep. We have followed too much the devices and desires of our own hearts. We have offended against thy holy laws. We have left undone those things which we ought to have done; And we have done those things which we ought not to have done; And there is no health in us. But thou, O Lord, have mercy upon us, miserable offenders. Spare thou those, O God, who confess their faults. Restore thou those who are penitent; According to thy promises declared unto mankind in Christ Jesus our Lord. And grant,

O most merciful Father, for his sake; That we may hereafter live a godly, righteous, and sober life, To the glory of thy holy Name. Amen.

The Declaration of Absolution, or Remission of Sins.

¶ To be made by the Priest alone, standing; the People still kneeling.

ALMIGHTY God, our heavenly Father, who of his great mercy hath promised forgiveness of sins to all those who, with hearty repentance and true faith, turn unto him; Have mercy upon you; pardon and deliver you from all your sins; confirm and strengthen you in all goodness; and bring you to everlasting life; through Jesus Christ our Lord. *Amen.*

¶ Then the Minister shall kneel, and say the Lord's Prayer: the People still kneeling, and repeating it with him.

OUR Father, who art in heaven, Hallowed be thy Name. Thy kingdom come. Thy will be done on earth, As it is

in heaven. Give us this day our daily
bread. And forgive us our trespasses, As
we forgive those who trespass against us.
And lead us not into temptation; But deliver us from evil: For thine is the kingdom, and the power, and the glory, for
ever and ever. Amen.

O Lord, open thou our lips.
Answer. And our mouth shall show
forth thy praise.

¶ Here, all standing up, the Minister shall say,

Glory be to the Father, and to the Son,
and to the Holy Ghost;
Answer. As it was in the beginning, is
now, and ever shall be, world without end.
Minister. Praise ye the Lord.
Answer. The Lord's name be praised.

¶ Then shall follow a Portion *of the Psalms, as they are
appointed, or one of the* Selections, *as they are set forth
by this church, with the Doxology as in the Morning
Service.*

SELECTIONS OF PSALMS,

TO BE USED INSTEAD OF THE PSALMS
FOR THE DAY, AT THE DISCRETION
OF THE MINISTER.

Selection First.

PSALM 19.　*Cæli enarrant.*

THE heavens declare the · *glory of* `
God :* and the firmament · *sheweth
his* · *handy-* · *work.*

One day · *telleth an-* · *other :* and one
night · *certi-* · *fieth an-* · *other.*

There is neither · *speech nor* · *language:*
but their · *voices are* · *heard a-* · *mong
them.*

Their sound is gone out into · *all=* ·
lands : and their words into the ·
ends= · *of the* · *world.*

(70)

In them hath he set a tabernacle · *for the · sun:* which cometh forth as a bridegroom out of his chamber * and rejoiceth <u>as</u> a · *giant to · run his · course.*

It goeth forth from the uttermost part of the heaven * and runneth about unto the <u>end</u> of · *it a- · gain:* and there is nothing hid · *from the · heat there- · of.*

The law of the LORD is an undefiled <u>law</u> con- · *verting the · soul:* the testimony of the LORD is sure * and giveth · *wisdom · unto the · simple.*

The statutes of the LORD are right * and re- · *joice the · heart:* the commandment of the LORD is pure * and giveth · *light un- · to the · eyes.*

The fear of the LORD is clean * and en- · *dureth for- · ever:* the judgments of the LORD are <u>true</u> and · *righteous · alto- · gether*

More to be desired are they than gold * <u>yea</u> than · *much fine · gold:*

sweeter also than honey · *and the* ·
honey- · *comb.*

Moreover by <u>them</u> is thy · *servant* ·
taught : and in keeping of them · *there*
is · *great re-* · *ward.*

Who can tell how oft · *he of-* · *fend-*
eth : O cleanse thou me · *from my* · *se-*
cret · *faults.*

Keep thy servant also <u>from</u> pre- ·
sumptuous · *sins :* lest they g<u>et</u> the do- ·
minion · *over* · *me.*

Let the words of my mouth * and
the meditation · *of my* · *heart :* be al<u>way</u>
ac- · *ceptable* · *in thy* · *sight ;*

O · = = · *Lord :* my · *strength and* ·
my Re- · *deemer.*

PSALM 24. *Domini est terra.*

THE earth is the LORD'S * and <u>all</u>
that · *therein* · *is :* the compass of
the <u>world</u> and · *they that* · *dwell there-* ·
in.

For he hath <u>founded</u> it up- · *on the* ·

seas : and prep<u>a</u>red · *it up-* · *on the* ·
floods.

Who shall ascend into the hill · *of
the* · *Lord :* or who shall rise up · *in
his* · *holy* · *place ?*

Even he that hath clean <u>hands</u> and a ·
pure= · *heart :* and he that hath not
lift up his mind unto vanity * nor <u>sworn</u>
to de- · *ceive his* · *neigh=* · *bour.*

He shall receive the blessing · *from
the* · *Lord :* and righteousness <u>from</u> the ·
God of · *his sal-* · *vation.*

This is the generation of · *them that* ·
seek him : even of <u>them</u> that · *seek thy* ·
face O · *Jacob.*

Lift up your heads O ye gates * and
be ye lift up * ye ever- · *lasting* · *doors :*
and the <u>King</u> of · *glory* · *shall come* · *in.*

Who <u>is</u> the · *King of* · *glory ?*   It is
the Lord strong and mighty * <u>e</u>ven
the · *Lord=* · *mighty in* · *battle.*

Lift up your heads O ye gates * and
be ye lift up ye <u>ev</u>er- · *lasting* · *doors :*

and the <u>King</u> of · *glory* · *shall come* · *in.*

Who <u>is</u> the · *King of* · *glory?* Even the LORD of hosts · *he is the* · *King of* · *glory.*

PSALM 103. *Benedic, anima mea.*

PRAISE the LORD · *O my* · *soul :* and all that is within me · *praise his* · *holy* · *Name.*

Praise the LORD · *O my* · *soul :* <u>and</u> for- · *get not* · *all his* · *benefits ;*

Who forgiveth · *all thy* · *sin :* and healeth · *all=* · *thine in-* · *firmities ;*

Who saveth thy life · *from de-* · *struc-tion :* and crowneth <u>thee</u> with · *mercy and* · *loving-* · *kindness ;*

Who satisfieth thy mouth · *with good* · *things :* making thee <u>young</u> and · *lusty* · *as an* · *eagle.*

The LORD executeth righeousness and · *judg=* · *ment :* for all <u>them</u> that · are op- · *pressed with* · *wrong.*

He shewed his ways · *unto · Moses :*
his works unto the · *children of · Isra-* ·
el.

The LORD is full of compassion and
mer= · *cy :* long-suffering · *and of*
great= · *goodness.*

He will not · *always be · chiding :*
neither keepeth · *he is · anger for-* ·
ever.

He hath not dealt with us · *after*
our · sins : nor rewarded us according ·
to our · wicked-·· *nesses.*

For look how high the heaven is in
comparison · *of the · earth :* so great
is his mercy also toward · *them that* ·
fear= · *him !*

Look how wide also the east is · *from*
the · west : so far hath he · *set our · sins*
from · us.

Yea like as a father pitieth · *his own*
children : even so is the LORD merciful
unto · *them that · fear=* · *him.*

For he knoweth whereof · *we are*

made : he remembereth · *that we · are but · dust.*

The days of <u>man</u> are · *but as · grass :* for he flourisheth as a · *flower · of the · field.*

For as soon as the wind goeth over it · *it is · gone :* and the place there<u>of</u> shall · *know it · no=== · more.*

But the merciful goodness of the Lord endureth for ever and ever upon <u>them</u> that · *fear=== · him :* and his righteousness upon · *children's · chil===· dren ;*

Even upon such as · *keep his · cove-nant :* and think upon <u>his</u> com- · *mand=== · ments to · do them.*

The Lord hath prepared his · *seat in · heaven :* and his <u>kingdom</u> · *ruleth · over · all.*

O praise the Lord * ye angels of his * <u>ye</u> that ex- *cel in · strength :* ye that fulfil his commandment * and <u>hearken</u> unto the · *voice=== · of his · word.*

O praise the Lord all · *ye his* · *hosts :*
ye servants of his that · *do his* · *pleas*= ·
ure.

O speak good of the Lord * all ye
works of his * in all places of · *his*
do- · *minion :* praise thou the · *Lord*= ·
O my · *soul.*

(Service continued on page 101.*)*

Selection Fifth.

PSALM I.   *Beatus vir, qui non abiit.*

BLESSED is the man that hath not walked in the counsel of the un- godly * nor <u>stood</u> in the · *way of* · *sin- ners :* and hath not <u>sat</u> in the · *seat=* · *of the* · *scornful.*

But his delight is in the law · *of the* · *Lord :* and in his law will he exer<u>cise</u> him- · *self=* · *day and* · *night.*

And he shall be like a tree planted by the · *water-* · *side :* that will bring <u>forth</u> his · *fruit=* · *in due* · *season.*

His leaf also · *shall not* · *wither :* and look * whatsoever he doeth · *it shall* · *pros =* · *per.*

As for the ungodly * it is not · *so with* · *them :* but they are like the chaff * which the wind scattereth away · *from the* · *face of the* · *earth.*

(78)

Therefore the ungodly shall not be able to stand · *in the · judgment :* neither the sinners in the <u>congre</u>- · *gation · of the · righteous.*

But the Lord knoweth the way · *of the · righteous :* and the <u>way</u> of the un- · *godly · shall= · perish.*

Psalm 15. *Domine, quis habitabit ?*

LORD who shall dwell · *in thy · taber-nacle :* or who shall <u>rest</u> up- · *on* thy · *holy · hill ?*

Even he that leadeth an · *uncor-rupt · life :* and doeth the thing which is right * and speaketh the · *truth=* · *from his · heart.*

He that hath used no deceit in his tongue * nor done evil · *to his · neigh-bour :* and <u>hath</u> not · *slander-* · *ed his · neighbour.*

He that setteth not by himself * but is lowly in · *his own · eyes :* and maketh <u>much</u> of · *them that · fear the · Lord.*

He that sweareth unto his neigh-
bour * and disappointeth · *him* == · *not:*
<u>though</u> it · *were to* · *his own* · *hin-
drance.*

He that hath not given his money
upon ·*usu-* · *ry:* nor taken re<u>ward</u> a- ·
gainst the · *inno-* · *cent.*

Whoso doeth · *these*== · *things:* shall ·
nev== · *er*== · *fall.*

PSALM 91.   *Qui habitat.*

WHOSO dwelleth under the de<u>fence</u>
of the · *Most*== · *High:* shall
a<u>bide</u> under the · *shadow of* · *the Al-* ·
mighty.

I will say unto the LORD * Thou art
my hope * and · *my strong-* · *hold:* my
God * in · *him*== · *will I* · *trust.*

For he shall deliver thee from the
snare · *of the* · *hunter:* and <u>from</u> the ·
noisome · *pesti-* · *lence.*

He shall defend thee under his
wings * and thou shalt be safe · *under*

his · feathers : his faithfulness and <u>truth</u> shall · *be thy · shield and · buckler.*

Thou shalt not be afraid for any · *ter-ror by · night :* <u>nor</u> for the · *arrow that · flieth by · day :*

For the pestilence that walketh in · *dark=· ness :* nor for the sickness that destroyeth · *in the · noon=· day.*

A thousand shall fall beside thee * and ten thousand at · *thy right · hand :* but it shall · *not come · nigh=· thee.*

Yea with thine <u>eyes</u> shalt · *thou be- · hold :* and <u>see</u> the re- · *ward of · the un- · godly.*

For thou LORD · *art my · hope :* thou hast set thine <u>house</u> of de- · *fence=· very · high.*

There shall no evil happen · *unto · thee :* neither shall any · *plague come · nigh thy · dwelling.*

For he shall give his angels charge · *over · thee :* to keep · *thee in · all thy · ways.*

They shall bear thee · *in their* · *hands :* that thou hurt not thy · *foot a-* · *gainst a* · *stone.*

· Thou shalt go up<u>on</u> the · *lion and* · *adder :* the young lion and the dragon shalt thou · *tread un-* · *der thy* · *feet.*

Because he hath set his love upon me * therefore will <u>I</u> de-· *liver* · *him :* I will set him up because · *he hath* · *known my* · *Name.*

He shall call upon me * and I will · *hear═* · *him :* yea I am with him in trouble * I will deliver him * and · *bring═* · *him to* · *honour.*

With long life will I · *satisfy* · *him :* and · *shew him* · *my sal-* · *vation.*

(Service continued on page 101*.)*

Selection Sixth.

BLESSED is he whose unrighteous-
ness · *is for-* · *given:* <u>and</u> whose ·
sin is · *cover-* · *ed.*

Blessed is the man unto whom the
LORD im- · *puteth no sin:* and in whose ·
spirit there · *is no* · *guile.*

I will acknowledge my sin · *unto* ·
thee: and mine unrighteousness · *have
I* · *not==* · *hid.*

I said * I will confess my <u>sins</u> un- ·
to the · *Lord:* and so thou forg<u>a</u><u>v</u>est
the · *wicked-ness* · *of my* · *sin:*

For this shall every one that is godly
make his prayer unto thee * in a time
when thou · *mayest be* · *found:* but in
the great water-floods · *they shall* · *not
come* · *nigh him.*

Thou art a place to hide me in * thou

shalt preserve · *me from · trouble :* thou
shalt compass me ab<u>out</u> with · *songs of
· de- liver- · ance.*

I will inform thee * and teach thee in
the way wherein · *thou shalt · go :* and
I will · *guide thee · with mine · eye.*

Great plagues rem<u>ain</u> for · *the un- ·
godly :* but whoso putteth his trust in
the LORD * mercy embraceth · *him on ·
every · side.*

Be glad O ye righteous * and rejoice · *in the · Lord :* and be joyful all
ye · *that are · true of · heart.*

PSALM 130.   *De profundis.*

OUT of the deep have I called <u>un</u>-
to · *thee O · Lord :* Lord · *hear═ ·
my═ · voice.*

O let thine <u>ears</u> con- · *sider · well :*
the · *voice of · my com- · plaint.*

If thou LORD * wilt be extreme to
mark what is · *done a- · miss :* O · *Lord
who · may a- · bide it ?*

For <u>there</u> is · *mercy with* · *thee :* <u>there-</u>
fore · *shalt=* · *thou be* · *feared.*

I look for the LORD * my <u>soul</u> doth ·
wait for · *him :* <u>in</u> his · *word=* · *is my* ·
trust.

My soul <u>flee</u>th un- · *to the* · *Lord :* before the morning watch * I <u>say</u> be- · *fore*
the · *morning* · *watch.*

O Israel trust in the LORD * for with
the LORD · *there is* · *mercy :* and with
<u>him</u> is · *plente-* · *ous re-* · *demption.*

And he shall redeem · *Isra-* · *el :*
from · *all=* · *his=* · *sins.*

PSALM 121.   *Levavi oculos meos.*

I WILL lift up mine <u>eyes</u> un- · *to the* ·
  hills : from · *whence com-* · *eth my* · *help*

My help cometh <u>even</u> · *from the*
Lord : <u>who</u> hath · *made=* · *heaven and*
earth.

He will not suffer thy foot · *to be*
moved : and <u>he</u> that · *keepeth thee* · *will*
not · *sleep.*

Behold * he that keepeth · *Isra-* · *el* : shall neither · *slum=* · *ber nor* · *sleep.*

The LORD himself · *is thy* · *keeper* : the LORD is thy de<u>fence</u> up- · *on thy* · *right=* · *hand* :

So that the sun shall not burn · *thee by* · *day* : <u>nei</u>ther the · *moon=* · *by=* · *night.*

The LORD shall preserve thee · *from all* · *evil* : yea it is even he · *that shall* · *keep thy* · *soul.*

The LORD shall preserve thy going out * <u>and</u> thy · *coming* · *in* : from this time · *forth for* · *ever-* · *more.*

(Service continued on page 101.*)*

Selection Seventh.

PSALM 23. *Dominus regit me.*

THE LORD · *is my* · *shepherd :* therefore · *can I* · *lack=* · *nothing.*

He shall feed me <u>in</u> a · *green=* · *pasture :* and lead me <u>forth</u> be- · *side the* ·
waters of · *comfort.*

<u>He</u> shall con- · *vert my* · *soul :* and
bring me forth in the paths of righteousness · *for his* · *Name's=* · *sake.*

Yea though <u>I</u> walk through the valley of the shadow of death * I will ·
fear no · *evil :* for thou art with me *
thy <u>rod</u> and thy · *staff=* · *comfort* · *me.*

Thou shall prepare a table before me
against <u>them</u> that · *trouble* · *me :* thou
hast anointed my head with oil · *and*
my · *cup shall be* · *full.*

But thy loving-kindness and mercy

(87)

shall follow me all the days · *of my* · *life :* and I will dwell in the house · *of the* · *Lord for-* · *ever.*

PSALM 34. *Benedicam Domino.*

I WILL alway give <u>thanks</u> un- · *to the* · *Lord :* his <u>praise</u> shall · *ever* be · *in my* · *mouth.*

My soul shall make her boast · *in the* · *Lord :* the humble shall <u>hear</u> there- · *of=* · *and be* · *glad.*

O <u>praise</u> the · *Lord with* · *me :* and let us <u>magni</u>- · *fy his* · *Name to-* · *gether.*

I sought the <u>LORD</u> and he · *heard=* · *me :* yea he delivered me · *out of* · *all my* · *fear.*

They had an eye unto <u>him</u> and were · *lighten-* · *ed :* <u>and</u> their · *faces were* · *not a-* · *shamed.*

Lo the poor crieth * and the LORD · *heareth* · *him :* yea and saveth him · *out of* · *all his* · *troubles.*

The angel of the LORD tarrieth round about <u>them</u> that · *fear·*= · *him :* <u>and</u> de- · *liv*= · *ereth* · *them.*

O taste and see how gra<u>ci</u>ous the · *Lord*= · *is :* blessed <u>is</u> the · *man that* · *trusteth* · *in him.*

O fear the LORD * <u>ye</u> that · *are his* · *saints :* for <u>they</u> that · *fear him* · *lack*= · *nothing.*

The lions do lack * and · *suffer* · *hun-ger :* but they who seek the LORD * shall want no manner of · *thing*= · *that is* · *good.*

Come ye children * and <u>hearken</u> · *un-to* · *me :* I will teach <u>you</u> the · *fear*= · *of the* · *Lord.*

What man is <u>he</u> that · *lusteth to* · *live :* <u>and</u> would · *fain*= · *see good* · *days ?*

<u>Ke</u>ep thy · *tongue from* · *evil :* and thy lips · *that they* · *speak no* · *guile.*

Eschew evil * and · *do*= · *good :* seek · *peace*= · *and en-* · *sue it.*

The eyes of the <u>LORD</u> are · *over the* ·

righteous : and his <u>ears</u> are · *open un-* ʼ
to their · *prayers.*

The countenance of the LORD is against <u>them</u> that · *do=* · *evil :* to root out the remembrance · *of them · from the · earth.*

The righteous cry * and the LORD · *heareth · them :* and delivereth them · *out of · all their · troubles.*

The LORD is nigh unto them that are <u>of</u> a · *contrite · heart :* and will save such as be · *of an · humble · spirit.*

Great are the troubles · *of the · righte- ous :* but the <u>LORD</u> de- · *livereth him · out of · all.*

He keepeth · *all his · bones :* so that not · *one of · them is · broken.*

But misfortune shall slay · *the un-* · *godly :* and they that hate the righteous · *shall be · deso-* · *late.*

The LORD delivereth the souls · *of his ·* *servants :* and all they that put their trust in <u>him</u> shall · *not be · desti-* · *tute.*

PSALM 65. *Te decet hymnus.*

THOU O God * art · *praised in* · *Sion :* and unto thee shall the vow be per<u>form</u>ed · *in Je-* · *rusa-* · *lem.*

<u>Thou</u> that · *hearest the* · *prayer :* <u>un</u>to · *thee shall* · *all flesh* · *come.*

My mis<u>deeds</u> pre- · *vail a-* · *gainst me :* O be thou merciful · *un==* · *to our* · *sins.*

Blessed is the man whom thou choosest * and receivest · *unto* · *thee :* he shall dwell in thy court * and shall be satisfied with the pleasures of thy house * even · *of thy* · *holy* · *temple.*

Thou shalt show us wonderful things in thy righteousness * O <u>God</u> of · *our sal-* · *vation :* thou that art the hope of all the ends of the earth * and of <u>them</u> that re- · *main in the* · *broad==* · *sea.*

Who in his strength setteth · *fast the* · *mountains :* <u>and</u> is · *girded a-* · *bout with* · *power.*

Who stilleth the <u>rag</u>ing · *of the* · sea :
and the noise of his waves * <u>and</u> the ·
madness · *of the* · *people.*

They also that dwell in the uttermost
parts of the earth * shall be afraid · *at
thy* · *tokens :* thou that makest the out-
goings of the <u>morn</u>ing and · *evening to* ·
praise= · *thee.*

Thou visitest the <u>earth</u> and · *blessest* · *it :* thou makest it · *very* · *plente-* ·
ous.

The river of <u>God</u> is · *full of* · *water :*
thou preparest their corn * for <u>so</u> thou
pro- · *videst* · *for the* · *earth.*

Thou waterest her furrows * thou
sendest rain into the little · *valleys
there-* · *of :* thou makest it soft with the
drops of rain * and · *blessest the* · *increase* · *of it.*

Thou crownest the year · *with thy* ·
goodness : <u>and</u> thy · *clouds*= · *drop*= ·
fatness.

They shall drop upon the dwellings

of the · *wilder-* · *ness :* and the little <u>hills</u>
shall re- · *joice on* · *every* · *side.*

The folds shall be · *full of* · *sheep :*
the valleys also shall stand so thick with
corn * that · *they shall* · *laugh and* · *sing.*

(Service continued on page 101.)

PSALM 8. *Domine, Dominus noster.*

O LORD our Governor * how excel-
lent is thy <u>Name</u> in · *all the · world :*
thou that hast <u>set</u> thy · *glory a- · bove
the · heavens.*

Out of the mouth of very babes and
sucklings hast thou ordained strength *
because of thine · *ene- · mies :* that thou
mightest still the enemy · *and== · the
a- · venger.*

For I will consider thy heavens * even
the works · *of thy · fingers :* the moon and
the stars · *which thou · hast or- · dained.*

What is man * that thou art · *mind-
ful of · him :* and the son of man · *that
thou · visit-est · him ?*

Thou madest him lower · *than the ·
angels :* to <u>crown</u> him with · *glo== · ry
and · worship.*

(94)

Thou makest him to have dominion of the works · *of thy* · *hands :* and thou hast put all things <u>in</u> sub- · *jection* · *under his* · *feet ;*

All · *sheep and* · *oxen :* <u>yea</u> and the · *beasts=* · *of the* · *field :*

The fowls of the air * and the fishes · *of the* · *sea :* and whatsoever walketh · *through the* · *paths of the* · *seas.*

O Lord our · *Gover-* · *nor :* how excellent is thy · *Name in* · *all the* · *world !*

Psalm 33. *Exultate, justi.*

REJOICE in the Lord · *O ye* · *righteous :* for it becometh <u>well</u> the · *just=* · *to be* · *thankful.*

<u>Praise</u> the · *Lord with* · *harp :* sing praises unto him with the <u>lute</u> and · *instru-ment* · *of ten* · *strings.*

Sing unto the Lord a · *new=* · *song :* sing praises lustily unto him · *with a* · *good=* · *courage.*

For the <u>word</u> of the · *Lord is* · *true* · and · *all his* · *works are* · *faithful.*

He loveth righteousness and · *judg=* · *ment:* the earth is <u>full</u> of the · *good-ness* · *of the* · *Lord.*

By the word of the LORD <u>were</u> the · *heavens* · *made:* and all the hosts of them <u>by</u> the · *breath=* · *of his* · *mouth.*

He gathereth the waters of the sea together * as it <u>were</u> up- · *on an* · *heap:* and layeth up the <u>deep</u> as · *in a* · *trea-sure* · *house.*

Let all the earth · *fear the* · *Lord:* stand in awe of him * all y<u>e</u> that · *dwell=* · *in the* · *world.*

For he sp<u>ake</u> and · *it was* · *done:* he com<u>man</u>ded · *and=.* · *it stood* · *fast.*

PSALM 147.   *Laudate Dominum.*

O PRAISE the Lord * for it is a good thing to sing <u>praises</u> un- · *to* our · *God:* yea a joyful and pleasant thing it · *is to be* · *thank=* · *ful.*

The LORD doth build <u>up</u> Je- · *rusa-* · *lem :* and gather together the out- · *casts* *of* · *Isra-* · *el.*

He healeth those that are · *broken* *in* · *heart :* and giveth medicine to · *heal* *their* · *sick=* · *ness.*

He telleth the number · *of the* · *stars :* and calleth them · *all=* · *by their* · *names.*

Great is our LORD * and great · *is* *his* · *power :* yea and his · *wisdom is* · *infi-* · *nite.*

The LORD setteth · *up the* · *meek :* and bringeth the ungodly · *down=* · *to the* · *ground.*

O sing unto the <u>LORD</u> with · *thanks=* · *giving :* sing praises up<u>on</u> the · *harp* *un-* · *to our* · *God :*

Who covereth the heaven with clouds * and prepareth rain · *for the* · *earth :* and maketh the grass to grow upon the mountains * and · *herb for the* · *use of* · *men :*

Who giveth <u>fodder</u> un- · *to the* · *cattle :*

and feedeth the young ravens that · *call
up-* · *on══* · *him.*

The LORD's delight is in <u>them</u> that ·
fear══ · *him :* <u>and</u> put their · *trust══* ·
in his · *mercy.*

Praise the LORD * <u>O</u> Je-· *rusa-· lem :*
<u>praise</u> thy · *God O* · *Si══* · *on.*

For he hath made fast the bars · *of
thy* · *gates :* and hath blessed thy · *children* · *within* · *thee.*

He maketh peace · *in thy* · *borders :*
and filleth thee · *with the* · *flour of* ·
wheat.

He sendeth forth his comma<u>ndme</u>nt
up- · *on══* · *earth :* and his word · *runneth* · *very* · *swiftly.*

He giveth · *snow like* · *wool :* and
scattered the · *hoar══* · *frost like* · *ashes.*

He casteth <u>forth</u> his · *ice like* · *morsels :*
who is able · *to a-* · *bide his* · *frost ?*

He sendeth out his <u>word</u> and · *melt-
eth* · *them :* he bloweth with his wind ·
and the · *waters* · *flow.*

He sheweth his word · *unto* · *Jacob :*
his statutes and ordinances · *unto* · *Isra-* ·
el.

He hath not dealt <u>so</u> with · *any* · *na-*
tion : neither have the <u>hea</u>then · *knowl-*
edge · *of his* · *laws.*

Psalm 57.   *Miserere mei, Deus.*

SET up thyself O God * a- · *bove the* ·
   heavens : and thy <u>glo</u>ry a- · *bove══* ·
all the · *earth.*

My heart is fixed O God * my · *heart*
is · *fixed :* <u>I</u> will · *sing══* · *and give* ·
praise.

Awake up my glory * awake · *lute*
and · *harp :* I myself · *will a-* · *wake*
right · *early.*

I will give thanks unto thee O Lord *
a- · *mong the* · *people :* and I will sing
<u>unto</u> · *thee a-* · *mong the* · *nations.*

For the greatness of thy mercy <u>reach</u>-
eth un- · *to the* · *heavens :* <u>and</u> thy · *truth*
un- · *to the* · *clouds.*

Set up thyself O God a- · *bove the* · *heavens :* and thy glory a- · *bove══* · all the · *earth.*

GLORIA IN EXCELSIS.

GLORY <u>be</u> to · *God on* · *high :* and on earth · *peace good* · *will towards* · *men.* We praise thee * we bless thee * we · *wor - ship* · *thee :* we glorify thee * we give <u>thanks</u> to · *thee for* · *thy great* · *glory.* O Lord God · *Heaven-ly* · *King :* <u>God</u> the · *Fa-ther* · *Al══* · *mighty.*

O Lord * the only begotten Son · *Je-sus* · *Christ :* O Lord God * <u>Lamb</u> of · *God· Son* · *of the* · *Father :* that takest a<u>way</u> the · *sins of the* · *world :* have · *mer-cy up-* · *on══* · *us.* Thou that takest a<u>way</u> the · *sins of the* · *world :* have · *mer-cy up-* · *on══* · *us.* Thou that takest a<u>way</u> the · *sins of the* · *world :* re- · *ceive══* · *our══* · *prayer.* Thou that sittest at the right <u>hand</u> of · *God the* · *Father :* have · *mer-cy up-* · *on*═ · *us.*

For thou · *only art* · *holy :* thou · *on-ly* · *art the* · *Lord.* Thou only O Christ * <u>with</u> the · *Ho-ly* · *Ghost :* art most <u>high</u> in the · *glory of* · *God the* · *Father.* · *A*═ · *men.*

¶ *Then shall be read a Lesson from the Old Testament.*
  ¶ *After which shall be said or sung the following Psalm :*

CANTATE DOMINO.

O SING unto the LORD a · *new*═ · *song :* for he hath · *done*═ · *marvel-lous* · *things.*

With his own right hand and <u>with</u> his · *ho - ly* · *arm :* <u>hath</u> he · *gotten him-* · *self the* · *victory.*

The LORD de<u>clar</u>ed · *his sal-* · *vation :* his righteousness hath he openly <u>show-</u>ed · *in the* · *sight of the* · *heathen.*

He hath remembered his mercy and truth <u>toward</u> the · *house of* · *Israel :* and all the ends of the world have <u>seen</u> the sal- · *va - tion* · *of our* · *God.*

Show yourselves joyful unto the Lord · *all ye* · *lands :* <u>sing</u> re- · *joice and* · *give*═ · *thanks.*

Praise the <u>Lord</u> up- · *on the* · *harp :* sing to the harp <u>with</u> a · *psalm*═ · *of thanks-* · *giving.*

With trumpets · *also and* · *shawms :* O show yourselves joy<u>ful</u> be- · *fore the* · *Lord the* · *King.*

Let the sea make a noise * and <u>all</u> that · *there-in* · *is :* the round <u>world</u> and · *they that* · *dwell there-* · *in.*

Let the floods clap their hands * and let the hills be joyful to<u>get</u>her be- · *fore the* · *Lord :* <u>for</u> he · *cometh to* · *judge the* · *earth.*

With righteousness <u>shall</u> he · *judge the* · *world :* and the · *peo - ple* · *with*═ · *equity.*

Glory be to the <u>F</u>ather · *and to the
Son :* and · *to the · Ho - ly · Ghost :*
As it was in the beginning ✳ is now ✳
and · *ever shall · be :* <u>world</u> without ·
end= · *A*= · *men.*

BONUM EST CONFITERI.

IT is a good thing to give <u>thanks</u> un- ·
  to the · Lord : and to sing praises
unto thy · *Name O · Most*= · *Highest :*
To tell of thy loving-kindness <u>early</u> ·
in the · morning : and of thy · *truth in
the · night*= · *season ;*
Upon an instrument of ten strings
<u>and</u> up- · *on the · lute :* upon a loud in-
strument · *and up-* · *on the · harp.*
For thou LORD hast made me glad ·
through thy · works : and I will rejoice in
giving praise for the <u>oper</u>- · *a - tions · of
thy · hands.*

Glory be to the <u>Fa</u>ther · *and to the* ·
Son : and · *to the* · *Ho - ly* · *Ghost :*

As it was in the beginning * is now *
and · *ever shall* · *be :* <u>world</u> without ·
end═ · *A*═ · *men.*

¶ *Then shall be read a Lesson from the New Testa-*
ment, and after that shall be sung or said this
Psalm.

DEUS MISEREATUR.

GOD be merciful <u>un</u>to · *us and* · *bless*
us : and show us the light of his
countenance <u>and</u> be · *merci - ful* · *unto* ·
us ;

That thy way <u>may</u> be · *known up - on* ·
earth : thy <u>sav</u>ing · *health a-* · *mong all* ·
nations.

Let the people praise · *thee O* · *God :*
<u>yea</u> let · *all the* · *peo - ple* · *praise thee.*

O let the nations rejoice · *and be* ·
glad : for thou shalt judge the folk

righteously * and g<u>overn</u> the · *na - tions* ·
up - on · *earth.*

Let the people praise · *thee O* · *God :*
y<u>ea</u> let · *all the* · *peo - ple* · *praise thee.*

Then shall the <u>earth</u> bring · *forth*
her · *increase :* and God * even <u>our</u> own ·
God shall · *give us his* · *blessing.*

<u>God</u> shall · *bless=* · *us :* and all the
ends <u>of</u> the · *world shall* · *fear=* · *him.*

Glory be to the <u>Fa</u>ther · *and to the* ·
Son : and · *to the* · *Ho -ly* · *Ghost :*

As it was in the beginning * is now *
and · *ever shall* · *be :* <u>world</u> without ·
end= · *A=* · *men.*

¶ *Or this:*

BENEDIC, ANIMA MEA.

PRAISE the LORD · *O my* · *soul :* and
    all that is within me · *praise his* ·
ho - ly · *Name.*

Praise the LORD · *O my* · *soul :* <u>and</u>
for- · *get not* · *all his* · *benefits :*

Who forgiveth · *all thy* · *sin :* and healeth · *all=* · *thine in-* · *firmities.*

Who saveth thy life · *from des-* · *truction :* and crowneth thee with · *mercy and* · *lov-ing-* · *kindness.*

O praise the LORD ye angels of his * ye that ex- · *cel in* · *strength :* ye that fulfil his commandment * and hearken unto the · *voice of* · *his=* · *word.*

O praise the LORD all · *ye his* · *hosts :* ye servants of his that · *do his* · *pleas=* · *ure.*

O speak good of the LORD * all ye works of his * in all places of · *his do-* · *minion :* praise thou the · *Lord=* · *O my* · *soul.*

Glory be to the Father · *and to the* · *Son :* and · *to the* · *Ho - ly* · *Ghost :*

As it was in the beginning * is now * and · *ever shall* · *be :* world without · *end=* · *A=* · *men.*

¶ *Then shall be said the Apostles' Creed by the Minister and the People, standing. And any Churches may omit the words,* He descended into hell, *or may, instead of them, use the words,* He went into the place of departed spirits, *which are considered as words of the same meaning in the Creed.*

I BELIEVE in God, the Father Almighty, Maker of heaven and earth:

And in Jesus Christ his only Son, our Lord; Who was conceived by the Holy Ghost, Born of the Virgin Mary; Suffered under Pontius Pilate, Was crucified, dead, and buried; He descended into hell, The third day he rose from the dead; He ascended into heaven, And sitteth on the right hand of God the Father Almighty; From thence he shall come to judge the quick and the dead.

I believe in the Holy Ghost; the Holy Catholic Church, The Communion of Saints; The Forgiveness of sins; the Resurrection of the body; And the Life everlasting. Amen.

¶ *And after that, these Prayers following, all devoutly kneeling: the Minister first pronouncing,*

The Lord be with you.

Answer. And with thy spirit.

Minister. Let us pray.

O Lord, show thy mercy upon us.

Answer. And grant us thy salvation.

Minister. O God, make clean our hearts within us.

Answer. And take not thy Holy Spirit from us.

¶ *Then shall be said the Collect for the day; after that the Collects and Prayers following.*

A Collect for Peace.

O GOD, from whom all holy desires, all good counsels, and all just works do proceed; Give unto thy servants that peace, which the world cannot give; that our hearts may be set to obey thy commandments, and also that by thee, we, being defended from the fear of our enemies, may pass our time in rest and quietness;

through the merits of Jesus Christ our Saviour. Amen.

A Collect for Aid against Perils.

O LORD, our Heavenly Father, by whose Almighty power we have been preserved this day; By thy great mercy defend us from all perils and dangers of this night; for the love of thy only Son, our Saviour, Jesus Christ. Amen.

A Prayer for the President of the United States, *and all in Civil Authority.*

O LORD, our Heavenly Father, the high and mighty Ruler of the Universe, who dost from thy throne behold all the dwellers upon earth; Most heartily we beseech thee with thy favor to behold and bless thy servant THE PRESIDENT OF THE UNITED STATES, and all others in authority; and so replenish them with the grace of thy Holy Spirit, that they may always incline to thy will, and walk in thy way.   Endue them plenteously with heavenly gifts; grant them in health and prosperity long to live; and finally, after this life, to attain everlasting joy and felicity; through Jesus Christ our Lord.   Amen.

A Prayer for the Clergy and People.

ALMIGHTY and everlasting God, from whom cometh every good and perfect gift; Send down upon our Bishops and other Clergy, and upon the Congregations committed to their charge, the healthful Spirit of thy grace; and, that they may truly please thee, pour upon them the continual dew of thy blessing.   Grant this, O Lord, for the honor of our Advocate and Mediator, Jesus Christ.   Amen.

A Prayer for all Conditions of Men.

O GOD, the Creator and Preserver of all mankind, we humbly beseech thee for all sorts and conditions of men; that thou wouldest be pleased to make thy ways known unto them, thy saving health unto all nations. More especially we pray for thy holy Church universal; that it may be so guided and governed by thy good Spirit, that all who profess and call themselves Christians may be led into the way of truth, and hold the faith in unity of spirit, in the bond of peace, and in righteousness of life. Finally, we commend to thy fatherly goodness all those who are any ways afflicted, or distressed, in mind, body, or estate; that it may please thee to comfort and relieve them, according to their several necessities; giving them patience under their sufferings, and a happy issue out of all their afflictions. And this we beg for Jesus Christ's sake. Amen.

A General Thanksgiving.

ALMIGHTY God, Father of all mercies, we, thine unworthy servants, do give thee most humble and hearty thanks for all thy goodness and loving-kindness to us, and to all men. We bless thee for our creation, preservation, and all the blessings of this life; but above all, for thine inestimable love in the redemption of the world by our Lord Jesus Christ; for the means of grace, and for the hope of glory. And, we beseech thee, give us that due sense of all thy mercies, that our hearts may be unfeignedly thankful, and that we may show forth thy praise, not only with our lips, but in our lives; by giving up ourselves to thy service, and by walking before thee in holiness and righteousness all our days; through Jesus Christ our Lord, to whom, with thee and the Holy Ghost, be all honor and glory, world without end.— Amen.

A Prayer of St. Chrysostom.

ALMIGHTY God, who hast given us grace at this time with one accord to make our common supplications unto thee; and dost promise that when two or three are gathered together in thy Name thou wilt grant their requests; Fulfil now, O Lord, the desires and petitions of thy servants, as may be most expedient for them; granting us in this world knowledge of thy truth, and in the world to come life everlasting. Amen.

2 *Cor.* xiii. 14.

THE grace of our Lord Jesus Christ, and the love of God, and the fellow-ship of the Holy Ghost, be with us all evermore. Amen.

Here endeth the Order of Evening Prayer.

Special Canticles or Anthems.

FOR USE IN PLACE OF THE SELECTIONS
OR BEFORE THE SERVICE.

CHRISTMAS DAY.

From PSALMS 45, 89, 110.

THY seat O God * en- · *dureth for* ·
ever : the sceptre of thy kingdom ·
is a · *right=* · *sceptre.*

Thou hast loved righteousness * and
hated in- · *iqui-* · *ty :* wherefore God *
even thy God * hath anointed thee with
the oil of · *gladness a-* · *bove thy* · *fel-
lows.*

My song shall be alway of the loving-kindness · *of the* · *Lord :* with my
mouth will I ever be shewing thy truth *
from one gener- · *ation* · *to an-* · *other.*

For I have said * Mercy shall be set

(114)

up for- · *ever :* thy <u>truth</u> shalt thou · *stablish* · *in the* · *heavens.*

The LORD is · *our de-* · *fence :* the Holy <u>One</u> of · *Is-rael* · *is our* · *King.*

Thou spakest sometimes in visions unto thy · *saints and* · *saidst :* I have laid help upon One that is mighty * I have exalted One · *chosen out* · *of the people.*

I will set his dominion also · *in the* · *sea :* <u>and</u> his · *right hand* · *in the* · *floods.*

And I will make <u>him</u> my · *First=* · *born :* higher than the · *kings=* · *of the* · *earth.*

The LORD <u>said</u> un- · *to my* · *Lord :* Sit thou on my right hand * until I <u>make</u> thine · *ene-* · *mies thy* · *footstool.*

The LORD shall send the rod of thy power · *out of* · *Sion :* be thou ruler * even in the <u>midst</u> a- · *mong thine* · *ene- mies.*

In the day of thy power * shall the people offer thee freewill 'offerings <u>with</u>

an · *holy* · *worship :* the dew of thy birth
is <u>of</u> the · *womb of the* · *morn⹀* · *ing.*

The LORD <u>sware</u> and will · *not re-* ·
pent : Thou art a Priest forever * after
the order · *of Mel-* · *chize-* · *dech.*

Glory be to the <u>Father</u> · *and to the* ·
Son : and · *to the* · *Ho - ly* · *Ghost :*

As it was in the beginning * is now *
and · *ever shall* · *be :* <u>world</u> without ·
end⹀ · *A⹀* · *men.*

II.

ISAIAH ix. 6, 7.

FOR unto <u>us</u> a · *child is* · *born :* unto ·
us a · *Son is* · *given :*

And the government shall be up- · *or*
His · *shoulder :* and his · *Name⹀* · *shall*
be · *called :*

Wonderful * Counsel<u>lor</u> * the ·
Mighty · *God :* the Everlasting · *Father*
the · *Prince of* · *Peace.*

Of the increase of His government

and peace *there* shall · *be no · end :*
upon the throne of *David · and up- · on*
his · kingdom :

To order it and to establish it with
judgment · *and with · justice :* from ·
henceforth · even for- · ever.

The zeal · *of the · Lord :* of · *Hosts*
will · perform · this.

EPIPHANY.

ARISE, * shine * *for* thy · *light is ·*
come : and the glory of the · *Lord*
is · risen up- · on thee.

The Gentiles shall · *come to thy · light :*
and *kings* to the · *brightness · of thy ·*
rising.

Break forth into singing all ye waste
places · *of the · earth :* for the LORD
hath comforted His people * He *hath*
re- · *deemed Je- · rusa- · lem.*

The LORD hath made bare His holy

arm in the <u>eyes</u> of · *all the* · *nations :*
and all the ends of the earth shall see
the sal- · *vation* · *of our* · *God.*

EASTER DAY.

CHRIST our passover is sacrificed ·
   for= · *us :* <u>therefore</u> · *let us* · *keep*
the · *feast :*
   Not with the old leaven * neither
with the leaven of · *malice and* · *wick-*
edness .· but with the unleavened bread ·
of sin-· ceri-· ty and · *truth.*

   CHRIST being raised from the dead ·
dieth no · *more :* death hath no <u>more</u>
do- · *min - ion* · *over* · *him.*
   For in that he died * he died <u>unto</u> ·
sin= · *once :* but in that he liveth * he ·
liv - eth · *un - to* · *God.*
   Likewise reckon ye also yourselves
to be dead indeed · *un - to* · *sin :* but

alive unto <u>God</u> through · *Je- sus* · *Christ*
our · *Lord.*

CHRIST is risen · *from the* · *dead :*
and become the first · *fruits of* · *them*
that · *slept.*

For <u>since</u> by · *man came* · *death:* by
man came also the <u>resur</u>- · *rec- tion* · *of*
the · *dead.*

For <u>as</u> in · *Adam all* · *die :* even so in
<u>Christ</u> shall · *all be* · *made a-* · *live.*

Glory be to the <u>Fa</u>ther · *and to the* ·
Son : and · *to the* · *Ho - ly* · *Ghost :*

As it was in the beginning * is now *
and · *ever shall* · *be :* <u>world</u> without ·
end= · *A=* · *men.*

———

ASCENSION DAY.

From PSALMS 24, 47.

LIFT up your heads O ye gates * and
be ye lift up * ye ever- · *lasting* ·

doors : and the <u>King</u> of · *glory* · *shall come* · *in.*

Who <u>is</u> the · *King of* · *glory :* The Lord strong and mighty * even the · *Lord=* · *mighty in* · *battle.*

Lift up your heads O ye gates * and be ye lift up * ye ever- · *lasting* · *doors :* and the <u>King</u> of · *glory* · *shall come* · *in.*

Who <u>is</u> the · *King of* · *glory :* Even the Lord of hosts * · *he is the* · *King of* · *glory.*   -

O clap your hands together · *all ye* · *people :* shout unto God <u>with</u> the · *voice of* · *tri=* · *umph.*

For the <u>Lord</u> most · *high is* · *terrible :* he is a great King · *over* · *all the* · *earth.*

God is gone up · *with a* · *shout :* the Lord with the · *sound of a* · *trum=* · *pet.*

Sing praises to God * sing · *prais =* · *es :* sing praises unto our · *King sing* · *prais=* · *es.*

God reigneth <u>o</u>ver the · *hea=* · *then :*

God sitteth upon the throne · *of his* ·
holi- · *ness.*

The princes of the people are gathered together * even the people of the
<u>God</u> of ·*Abra-*· *ham :* for the shields of
the earth belong unto God * <u>he</u> is
greatly ex- · *alt=* · *ed.* ·

Glory be to the <u>Fa</u>ther · *and to the* ·
Son : and · *to the* · *Ho - ly* · *Ghost :*

As it was in the beginning * is now *
and · *ever shall* · *be :* <u>world</u> without ·
end= · *A=* · *men.*

WHIT-SUNDAY.

From Psalms 2, 68.

I WILL declare the decree * the Lord
hath said · *unto* · *me :* Thou art my
Son * this day have · *I be-* · *gotten* · *thee.*

Desire of me * and I shall give thee
the heathen for <u>thine</u> in- · *herit-* · *ance :*

and the utmost <u>parts</u> of the · *earth for* ·
thy pos- · *session*

Be wise now <u>therefore</u> · *O ye* · *kings :*
be instructed * ye · *judges* · *of the* ·
earth.

<u>Serve</u> the · *Lord with* · *fear :* <u>and</u>
re- ·. *joice══* · *with══* · *trembling.*

Sing unto God * sing <u>praises</u> · *to his* ·
Name : extol him that rideth upon the
heavens by his name JAH * <u>and</u> re- ·
joice be- · *fore══* · *him.*

Thou O God sentest a gracious rain
upon <u>thine</u> in- · *herit-* · *ance :* and re-
freshedst · *it when* · *it was* · *weary.*

The LORD · *gave the* · *word :* great
was the company of · *those that* · *pub-*
lished · *it.*

Though ye have <u>lain</u> a- · *mong the* · *pots:*
yet shall ye be as the wings of a dove
covered with silver * <u>and</u> her · *feathers*
with · *yellow* · *gold.*

Thou hast ascended on high * thou
hast led captivity captive * thou hast

received · *gifts for · men :* yea for the rebellious also * that the LORD · *God might · dwell a- · mong them.*

Blessed be the LORD * who daily loadeth us with · *bene- · fits :* even the · *God of · our sal- · vation.*

Sing unto God * ye kingdoms · *of the · earth :* O sing · *praises un- · to the · Lord :*

To him that rideth upon the heaven of heavens * which · *were of · old :* lo he doth send out his voice * and · *that a · mighty · voice.*

Ascribe ye strength · *unto · God :* his excellency is over Israel * and his · *strength is · in the · clouds.*

O God * thou art terrible out of thy · *holy · places :* the God of Israel is he that giveth strength and power unto his people. * · *Bless= · ed be · God.*

Glory be to the Father · *and to the · Son :* and · *to the · Ho - ly · Ghost :*

As is was in the beginning * is now *

and · *ever shall* · *be :* <u>world</u> without
end= · *A=* · *men.*

———

TE DEUM LAUDAMUS.

WE praise · *thee O* · *God :* we acknowledge · *thee to* · *be the* · *Lord.*
All the <u>earth</u> doth · *worship* · *thee :*
the · *Father* · *ever-* · *lasting.*

To thee all <u>An</u>gels · *cry a-* · *loud :* the
<u>Hea</u>vens and · *all the* · *Powers there-* ·
in.

To thee <u>Che</u>rubim and · *Seraph-* · *im :*
con- · *tinual-* · *ly do* · *cry :*

<u>Ho</u>ly · *Ho-ly* · *Holy :* Lord · *God of* ·
Saba- · *oth ;*

<u>Hea</u>ven and · *earth are* · *full :* of the
Majesty · *of thy* · *Glo=* · *ry.*

The glorious company of the A- ·
pos= · *tles :* praise · *= =* · *= =* · *thee.*

The goodly fellowship <u>of</u> the · *Pro=*
phets : praise · *= =* · *= =* · *thee.*

The noble <u>ar</u>my of · *Mar=* · *tyrs :*
praise · = = · = = · *thee.*

The Holy Church throughout · *all
the* · *world :* doth · *=ac-* · *knowledge* ·
Thee.

The · *Fa=* · *ther :* <u>of</u> an · *infinite* ·
Majes- · *ty ;*

Thine adorable * <u>true</u> and · *only* ·
Son : also the <u>Holy</u> · *Ghost the* · *Com-
fort-* · *er.*

Thou <u>art</u> the · *King of* · *Glory :* O ·
= = · = = · *Christ ;*

Thou art the <u>ev</u>er- · *lasting* · *Son :* of
=the · *Fa=* · *ther.*

When thou tookest upon thee <u>to</u> de-
liver · *man :* thou didst humble thy<u>self</u>
to be · *born=* · *of a* · *Virgin.*

When thou hadst over<u>come</u> the ·
sharpness of · *death :* thou didst open
the Kingdom of <u>Hea</u>ven to · *all be-* ·
liev= · *ers.*

Thou sittest at the right · *hand of
God :* <u>in</u> the · *Glory* · *of the* · *Father.*

We believe that · *Thou shalt* · *come :* to · *be͇* · *our͇* · *Judge.*

We therefore pray thee · *help thy* · *servants :* whom thou hast redeemed · *with thy* · *precious* · *blood.*

Make them to be numbered · *with thy* · *Saints :* in · *glory* · *ever-* · *lasting.*

O Lord · *save thy* · *people :* and · *bless͇* · *thine͇* · *heritage.*

G · *overn* · *them :* and · *lift them* · *up for* · *ever.*

Day · *͇by* · *day :* we · *magni-* · *fy͇* · *thee ;*

And we · *worship thy* · *Name :* ever · *world with-* · *out͇* · *end.*

Vouch- · *safe O* · *Lord :* to keep us this · *day with-* · *out͇* · *sin.*

O Lord have mercy up- · *on͇* · *us :* have · *mercy* · *upon* · *us.*

O Lord let thy mercy · *be up-* · *on us :* as our · *trust is* · *in͇* · *thee.*

O Lord in thee · *have I* · *trusted :* let me · *never* · *be con-* · *founded.*

BENEDICITE, OMNIA OPERA DOMINI.

O ALL ye Works of the Lord * bless ·
ye the · Lord: praise him and ·
magni- fy · him for- · ever.

O ye Angels of the LORD * bless · ye
the · Lord: praise him, &c.

O ye Heavens * bless · ye the · Lord:
praise him, &c.

O ye Waters that be above the firmament * bless · ye the · Lord: praise him,
&c.

O all ye Powers of the LORD * bless ·
ye the · Lord: praise him, &c.

O ye Sun and Moon * bless · ye the ·
Lord: praise him, &c.

O ye Stars of Heaven * bless · ye the ·
Lord: praise him, &c.

O ye Showers and Dew * bless · ye
the · Lord: praise him, &c.

O ye Winds of God * bless · ye the ·
Lord: praise him, &c.

O ye Fire and Heat * bless · *ye the Lord:* praise him, &c.

O ye Winter and Summer * bless · *ye the · Lord:* praise him, &c.

O ye Dews and Frosts * bless · *ye the · Lord:* praise him, &c.

O ye Frost and Cold * bless · *ye the · Lord:* praise him, &c.

O ye Ice and Snow * bless · *ye the · Lord:* praise him, &c.

O ye Nights and Days * bless · *ye the · Lord:* praise him, &c.

O ye Light and Darkness * bless · *ye the · Lord:* praise him, &c.

O ye Lightnings and Clouds * bless · *ye the · Lord:* praise him, &c.

O let the Earth · *bless the · Lord:* yea let it praise him and · *magni - fy · him for- · ever.*

O ye Mountains and Hills * bless · *ye the · Lord:* praise him, &c.

O all ye Green Things upon the earth * bless · *ye the · Lord:* praise him, &c.

O ye Wells * bless · *ye the* · *Lord :* praise him, &c.

O ye Seas and Floods * bless · *ye the* · *Lord :* praise him, &c.

O ye Whales and all that move in the waters * bless · *ye the* · *Lord :* praise him, &c.

O all ye Fowls of the Air * bless · *ye the* · *Lord :* praise him, &c.

O all ye Beasts and Cattle * bless · *ye the* · *Lord :* praise him, &c.

O ye Children of Men * bless · *ye the* · *Lord :* praise him, &c.

O let Israel · *bless the* · *Lord :* praise him, &c.

O ye Priests of the LORD * bless · *ye the* · *Lord :* praise him, &c.

O ye Servants of the LORD * bless · *ye the* · *Lord :* praise him, &c.

O ye Spirits and Souls of the Righteous * bless · *ye the* · *Lord :* praise him, &c.

O ye holy and humble Men of heart * bless · *ye the* · *Lord :* praise him, &c.

Glory be to the <u>Fa</u>ther · *and to the*
Son : and · *to the* · Ho - ly · Ghost :

As it was in the beginning * is now *
and · *ever shall · be :* <u>world</u> without ·
end== · *A*== · *men.*

GLORIA CHRISTI.

O SING unto the <u>Lord</u> a · *new*== ·
song : let the congregation of ·
saints== · *praise*== · *Him.*

Let Israel rej<u>oice</u> in · *Him that · made
him :* and let the children of Zion be · *joyful · in their · King.*

In <u>Him</u> * the · *First and the · Last :*
the same yester<u>day</u> * to- · *day*== · *and
for-* · *ever.*

The <u>Angel</u> · *of the · Covenant :* the ·
Ancient · of== · *days.*

The desire · *of all · nations :* the
<u>Glory</u> · *of His · people · Israel.*

The <u>Root</u> and · *Offspring of · David:* The · *Bright and · Morning · Star.*

The · *Son of · Mary:* The Only Begotten of the F<u>ATHER</u> · *full of · grace and · truth.*

The <u>D</u>ay Spring · *from on · High:* The Sun of Rightcousness risen with · *healing · in His · wings.*

The · *Rose of · Sharon:* <u>and</u> the · *Lily · of the · Valley.*

The · *Crown of · Glory:* The Diadem of · *Beauty un-* · *to His · people.*

The Author and Finisher · *of our · Faith:* the Shepherd and · *Bishop · of our · souls.*

The Lamb slain from the foundation · *of the · world:* High Priest forever * after the · *order · of Mel-* · *chizedec.*

The Propitiation <u>for</u> the · *Sins of the · world:* the Only Name under Heaven given among men where- · *by we · must be · saved.*

The <u>Pro</u>phet · *Priest and* · *King :*
The · *Lord our* · *Righteous-* · *ness.*   ·

The Judge <u>of</u> the · *Quick and the* ·
Dead : He that <u>hath</u> the · *keys of* ·
Death and · *Hell.*

God manifest · *in the* · *Flesh :* Image ·
of the In- · *visible* · *God.*

The Brightness <u>of</u> The · *Father's* ·
Glory : The express · *Image* · *of His* ·
Person.

King of <u>King</u>s * and · *Lord of* ·
Lords : God over all · *blessed for* ·
ever- · *more.*

THE BEATITUDES.

MATTHEW V.

BLESSED <u>are</u> the · *poor in* · *spirit :*
for theirs is the · *Kingdom* · *of═* ·
Heaven.

Blessed are · *they that* · *mourn :* for ·
· *they shall* · *be ═* · *comforted.*

<u>Bless</u>ed · *are the · meek :* for they · *shal' in- · herit the · earth.*

Blessed are they which do hunger and thirst · *after · righteousness :* for · *they shall · be= · filled.*

<u>Bless</u>ed · *are the · merciful :* for they · *shall ob- · tain= · mercy.*

Blessed <u>are</u> the · *pure in · heart :* for · *they shall · see= · God.*

Blessed <u>are</u> the · *peace- = · makers :* for they shall be · *called the · children of · God.*

Blessed are they which are persecuted for · *righteousness' · sake :* for theirs i<u>s</u> the · *Kingdom · of= · Heaven.*

MAGNIFICAT.

M Y soul doth <u>magn</u>i- · *fy the · Lord :* and my spirit hath re- · *joiced in · God my · Saviour.*

For he hath re- · *garded the · lowli- ness :* of · *His= · hand== · maiden ;*

For behold · *from hence-* · *forth :* all generations · *shall=* · *call me* · *blessed.*

For he that is mighty hath magnified me * and <u>ho</u>ly · *is His* · *Name :* and His mercy is on them that fear Him * through- · *out all* · *gene-* · *rations.*

He hath shewed strength · *with His* · *arm :* He hath scattered the proud in the im<u>a</u>gi- · *nation* · *of their* · *hearts.* .

He hath put down the m<u>igh</u>ty · *from their* · *seats :* and hath exalt<u>ed</u> the · *humble* · *and the* · *meek.*

He hath filled the <u>hun</u>gry · *with good* · *things :* and the rich He hath · *sent=* · *empty a-* · *way.*

He * remembering his mercy * hath holpen His · *servant* · *Israel :* as He promised to our forefathers * Abraham · *and his* · *seed for* · *ever.*

III.

HYMNAL.

I.—THE CHRISTIAN YEAR.

ADVENT.

1. 8s. 7s. 4. *(Hymnal 1.)*

L O, He comes, with clouds descending,
 Once for favored sinners slain;
Thousand thousand saints attending,
 Swell the triumph of His train :
 ‖: Hallelujah ! :‖
God appears on earth to reign.

2 Yea, Amen ; let all adore Thee,
 High on Thine eternal throne ;
Saviour, take the power and glory ;
 Claim the kingdom for Thine own ;
 ‖: O come quickly ! :‖
Hallelujah ! Come, Lord, come. Amen.

2.

W HEN He cometh, when He cometh,
 To make up His jewels;
All His jewels, precious jewels,
 His lov'd and His own.

3

Chorus.—Like the stars of the morning,
    His bright crown adorning;
    They shall shine in their beauty,
    Bright gems for His crown.

2 He will gather, He will gather,
  The gems for His kingdom;
All the pure ones, all the bright ones,
  His lov'd and His own.—*Chorus.*

3 Little children, little children,
  Who love their Redeemer,
Are the jewels, precious jewels,
  His loved and His own.—*Chorus.*   Amen.

3.   *7s., double.*   *(Hymnal* 43.)

WATCHMAN ! tell us of the night,
  What its signs of promise are.
  Traveller ! o'er yon mountain's height,
  See that glory-beaming star.
Watchman ! does its beauteous ray
Aught of joy or hope foretell ?
  Traveller ! yes, it brings the day,
  Promised day of Israel.

2 Watchman ! tell us of the night;
  Higher yet that star ascends.
    Traveller ! blessedness and light,
    Peace and truth its course portends.

Watchman ! will its beams alone
Gild the spot that gave them birth ?
    Traveller ! Ages are its own ;
    See, it bursts all o'er the earth.

3 Watchman ! tell us of the night,
For the morning seems to dawn.
    Traveller ! darkness takes its flight ;
    Doubt and terror are withdrawn.
Watchman ! let thy wanderings cease ;
Hie thee to thy quiet home.
    Traveller ! lo, the Prince of Peace,
    Lo ! the Son of God is come.   Amen.

4.   *C. M.*   *(Hymnal 15.)*

HARK! the glad sound ! the Saviour comes,
    The Saviour promised long :
Let every heart prepare a throne,
    And every voice a song.

2 He comes the prisoners to release,
    In Satan's bondage held ;
The gates of brass before Him burst,
    The iron fetters yield.

3 He comes the broken heart to bind,
    The bleeding soul to cure,
And with the treasures of His grace,
    To enrich the humble poor.

4 Our glad Hosannas, Prince of Peace,
   Thy welcome shall proclaim ;
And heaven's eternal arches ring
   With Thy beloved Name.   Amen.

5.   8s. 7s.   *(Hymnal 16.)*

HAIL ! Thou long expected Jesus,
   Born to set Thy people free ;
From our sins and fears release us,
   Let us find our rest in Thee.

2 Israel's strength and consolation,
   Hope of all the earth Thou art ;
Long desired of every nation,
   Joy of every waiting heart.

3 Born Thy people to deliver,
   Born a child, yet God our King,
Born to reign in us for ever,
   Now Thy gracious kingdom bring.

4 By Thine own eternal Spirit,
   Rule in all our hearts alone ;
By Thine all-sufficient merit,
   Raise us to Thy glorious throne.   Amen.

CHRISTMAS.

6. *(Hymnal 23.)*

Chor.—Shout the glad tidings, exultingly sing;
    Jerusalem triumphs, Messiah is King !

ZION, the marvellous story be telling,
    The Son of the Highest, how lowly His
      birth !
The brightest archangel in glory excelling,
He stoops to redeem thee, He reigns upon
      earth.
Chor.—Shout the glad tidings, exultingly sing ;
    Jerusalem triumphs, Messiah is King !
    Shout the glad tidings, exultingly sing ;
    Jerusalem triumphs, Messiah is King !
    Messiah is King ! Messiah is King !

2 Tell how He cometh ; from nation to nation,
The heart-cheering news let the earth echo
      round ;
How free to the faithful He offers salvation,
How His people with joy everlasting are
      crown'd.—*Chorus.*

3 Mortals, your homage be gratefully bringing,
And sweet let the gladsome Hosanna arise ;
Ye angels the full Hallelujah be singing ;
One chorus resound through the earth and the
      skies.—*Chorus,* AMEN.

7   *C. M.*   *(Hymnal 18.)*

WHILE shepherds watch'd their flocks by
     night,
   All seated on the ground,
The angel of the Lord came down,
   And glory shone around.

2 *" Fear not,"* said he, for mighty dread,
     Had seized their troubled mind ;
  " Glad tidings of great joy I bring
     To you and all mankind.

3 *" To you in David's town, this day*
     Is born of David's line,
  The Saviour, Who is Christ the Lord,
     And this shall be the sign :

4 *" The heavenly Babe you there shall find*
     To human view display'd,
  All meanly wrapped in swathing bands,
     And in a manger laid."

5 Thus spake the seraph ; and forthwith
     Appeared a shining throng
  Of angels, praising God, and thus
     Address'd their joyful song :

6 *" All glory be to God on high,*
     And to the earth be peace ;
  Good-will, henceforth, from heaven to man
     Begin and never cease."   AMEN.

8.

Y E angels in glory,
Repeat the glad story
Ye brought to the shepherds on Bethlehem's
morn ;
When the voice of your singing
From Heaven came, bringing
The tidings that Jesus, the Saviour, was
born.

Chorus.—O, chorus of fire !
Burst forth from God's choir !
Let the loud Hallelujahs awaken the morn,
Till the flowers on the hills,
And the waves in the rills,
All tremble with joy that the Saviour is born.

2 From His throne condescending,
In wondrous love bending,
He comes to redeem us, to dwell upon earth ;
And the heavenly chorus
In rapture swells o'er us,
And angels come gladly to herald His birth.
—*Chorus.*

3 We praise Thee for ever,
Christ born to deliver ;
We praise Thee, we bless Thee, we magnify
Thee !
All earth shall confess Thee

And joyfully bless Thee,
And join in glad rapture with Heaven's harmony.
—Chorus.

4 By the star's sure revealing
The wise men are kneeling,
As, lowly adoring, their treasures they fling ;
And we, with glad voices,
While Heaven's choir rejoices,
Like them, to the Saviour our offerings will
bring.—*Chorus.*

5 Each heart, with joy swelling,
God's mercy is telling,
While the song of the angels re-echoes again ;
To the Saviour who sought us,
For the love that He brought us,
Be glory for ever ! Hallelujah ! Amen !
.—*Chorus.* AMEN.

9

SILENT night ! Holy night !
All is calm, all is bright ;
Round yon Virgin Mother and Child.
Holy Infant, so tender and mild,
‖: Sleep in heavenly peace. ‖

2 Silent night ! Holy night !
Shepherds quake at the sight !

Glories stream from heaven afar,
Heavenly hosts sing Alleluia!
　　　‖: Christ, the Saviour is born ! :‖

3 Silent night ! Holy night !
Son of God ; love's pure light,
Radiant beams from Thy holy face
With the dawn of redeeming grace,
　　　‖: Jesus, Lord, at thy birth ! :‖　Amen.

10.

WONDERFUL night ! Wonderful night !
　Angels and shining immortals,
Thronging thine ebony portals,
Fling out their banners of light :
Wonderful, wonderful night !

2 Wonderful night ! Wonderful night !
Dreamed of by prophets and sages !
Manhood redeemed for all ages,
Welcomes thy hallowing might,
Wonderful, wonderful night !

3 Wonderful night ! Wonderful night !
Down o'er the stars to restore us,
Leading His flame-winged chorus,
Comes the Eternal to sight :
Wonderful, wonderful night !

4 Wonderful night ! Wonderful night !
Sweet be thy rest to the weary,

Making the dull heart and dreary
Laugh in a dream of delight :
Wonderful, wonderful night !

5 Wonderful night ! Wonderful night !
Let me, as long as life lingers,
Sing with the cherubim singers,
" Glory to God in the height :"
Wonderful, wonderful night !   Amen.

11.

CHRIST is born, and heaven rejoices,
   Judah's plain is bathed in light ;
Thousand thousand harps and voices
   Break the silence of the night.
Chorus.—Glory in the highest, glory,
     Peace on earth, good-will to men ;
     Glory in the highest, glory,
     Peace on earth, good-will to men.

2 Christ is born, the Lord's Anointed
   Leaves the heavenly world awhile,
Enters on the work appointed,
   God and man to reconcile.—*Chorus.*

3 To the lost He brings salvation,
   Freedom to the captive slave ;
Peace amid death's desolation,
   Victory o'er the boasting grave.—*Chorus.*

4 Christ is born, oh, wondrous story!
   Lord of life, yet born to die ;
 Sorrow's child, yet King of glory ;
   Born to rule and reign on high.—*Chorus.*

5. Royal Babe, tho' few enthrone Him,
   Few their grateful offerings bring ;
 All the tribes of earth shall own Him,
   Prince of peace, creation's King.—*Chorus.*

AMEN.

12.

THE city's hum was hush'd and still,
   And silence reign'd o'er vale and hill ;
 The birds had sought the sheltering tree,
   The flocks were folded tenderly ;
 No sound of life was on the breeze
   That murmured thro' the olive-trees,
 And, 'mid the stars, heaven's brightest gem
   Shone over sleeping Bethlehem.

Chorus.—Good tidings, good tidings,
         Good tidings of great joy!
         On this blest morn
         A Prince is born!
         Good tidings of great joy!
 The Prince of peace, the Incarnate Word,
   A Saviour, Christ the Lord !

13

Glory to God in the highest, then,
Glory to God in the highest,
And on earth peace, good-will to men

2 In rapturous tone that strain arose,
And burst upon the night's repose;
A white-robed legion from on high
With dazzling glory filled the sky;
The music of the angel band
Went floating o'er the holy land,
While on the listening shepherd's ear
Still rang that chorus loud and clear.

—Chorus.

3 The vision faded from the sight,
Hushed were those voices of the night,
And brightly dawned upon the earth
The morning of our Saviour's birth;
Oh morn of gladness, day of joy,
Well may thy praise our tongues employ!
Well may we join that song of love
First sung by minstrels from above.

—Chorus. AMEN

13. *(Hymnal 19.)*

O COME, all ye faithful,
Joyful and triumphant:
O come ye, O come ye to Bethlehem;
Come and behold Him

Born, the King of Angels ;
O come, let us adore Him,
O come let us adore Him,
O come let.us adore Him, Christ the Lord.

2 Sing, choirs of angels,
Sing in exultation,
Sing, all ye citizens of heaven above :
Glory to God
In the highest ;
O come, let us adore Him,
O come, let us adore Him,
O come let us adore Him, Christ the Lord.

3 Yea, Lord, we greet Thee,
Born this happy morning ;
Jesus, to Thee be glory given ;
Word of the Father,
Now in flesh appearing :
O come, let us adore Him,
O come, let us adore Him,
O come, let us adore Him, Christ the Lord.

Amen

14.　　　　　　　*8s. 7s. 4.*　　　　*(Hymnal 24.*

ANGELS, from the realms of glory,
Wing your flight o'er all the earth ;
Ye who sang creation's story,
Now proclaim Messiah's birth :

15

CHRISTMAS.

‖: Come and worship, :‖
Worship Christ, the new-born King.

Shepherds in the field abiding,
  Watching o'er your flocks by night ;
God with man is now residing,
  Yonder shines the infant-light :
    ‖: Come and worship, :‖
    Worship Christ, the new-born King.

Sages, leave your contemplations ;
  Brighter visions beam afar :
Seek the great Desire of nations,
  Ye have seen His natal star:
    ‖: Come and worship, :‖
    Worship Christ, the new-born King.

Saints before the altar bending,
  Watching long in hope and fear,
Suddenly the Lord, descending,
  In His temple shall appear:
    ‖: Come and worship, :‖
    Worship Christ the new-born King.
              AMEN.

EPIPHANY.

15. 7s. 6s., *double.* *(Hymnal* 34.*)*

HAIL to the Lord's Anointed,
　　Great David's greater Son!
Hail, in the time appointed,
　　His reign on earth begun!
He comes to break oppression,
　　To set the captive free,
To take away transgression,
　　And rule in equity.

2 He comes with succour speedy,
　　To those who suffer wrong,
To help the poor and needy,
　　And bid the weak be strong;
To give them songs for sighing,
　　Their darkness turn to light,
Whose souls, condemned and dying,
　　Were precious in His sight.

3 He shall descend like showers
　　Upon the fruitful earth,
And love and joy, like flowers,
　　Spring in His path to birth:
Before Him on the mountains,
　　Shall peace, the herald, go ;
And righteousness, in fountains,
　　From hill to valley flow.

4 To Him shall prayer unceasing,
  And daily vows ascend ;
His kingdom, still increasing,
  A kingdom without end :
The tide of time shall never
  His covenant remove ;
His name shall stand forever ;
  That name to us is Love.   Amen.

16   *6s. 5s., double.*

IN the wintry heaven,
    Shines a wondrous star ;
In the East, the wise men
    Watch it from afar,
Asking : " *What this lustre,*
    So unearthly bright ? "
Answering : " *Christ in glory*
    Comes to earth to-night."

2 O'er the dusty highways,
    O'er the deserts drear,
From the East, the wise men
    Watch it shining clear ;
Asking : " *Shall we follow*
    In this star-lit way ? "
Answering : " *Yes, 'twill lead us*
    To the perfect day.

3 In a lowly manger
    Lies an Infant weak ;
Is it He whom wise men
    Come so far to seek ?
Asking : " *Where the Monarch ?*
    Where Judea's King ? "
Saying : " *Gifts and worship*
    To His throne we bring. "

4 In our hearts, we children
    See this star once more—
Not as wise men saw it
    In the days of yore—
Asking : " *May we bring Him*
    Children's love to-day ? "
Answering : " *Come, dear children,*
    Jesus says we may. "　　A MEN.

17.　　　　*8s. 7s., double.*

SAW ye never in the twilight,
    When the sun had left the skies,
Up in heav'n the clear stars shining,
    Thro' the gloom, like silver eyes ?
So of old, the wise men watching,
    Saw a little stranger star,
And they knew the King was given,
    And they followed it from far.

2 Heard ye never of the story,
   How they cross'd the desert wild,
Journey'd on by plain and mountain,
   Till they found the Holy Child?
How they open'd all their treasure,
   Kneeling to that Infant King,
Gave the gold and fragrant incense,
   Gave the myrrh in offering.

3 Know ye not that lowly Baby
   ' Was the bright and morning Star,
He who came to light the Gentiles
   And the darkened isles afar?
And we too may seek His cradle
   There our hearts' best treasures bring,
Love, and faith, and true devotion,
   For our Saviour, God, and King.   AMEN.

18.   *Six 7s.*   *(Hymnal 45.)*

AS with gladness men of old
   Did the guiding-star behold;
As with joy they hail'd its light,
Leading onward, beaming bright;
So, most gracious Lord, may we
Evermore be led to Thee.

2 As with joyful steps they sped
   To that lowly manger-bed;

There to bend the knee before
Him Whom heaven and earth adore,
So may we with willing feet
Ever seek the mercy-seat.

3 As they offered gifts most rare
At that manger rude and bare ;
So may we with holy joy,
Pure and free from sin's alloy,
All our costliest treasures bring,
Christ! to Thee, our Heavenly King.

4 Holy Jesu, every day
Keep us in the narrow way ;
And, when earthly things are past,
Bring our ransom'd souls at last
Where they need no star to guide,
Where no clouds Thy glory hide.

5 In the heavenly country bright
Need they no created light ;
Thou its Light, its Joy, its Crown,
Thou its Sun which goes not down ;
There for ever may we sing
Alleluias to our King.   AMEN.

9.   *(Hymnal 37.)*

BRIGHTEST and best of the sons of the
morning,
Dawn on our darkness, and lend us Thine aid.

Star of the east, the horizon adorning,
  Guide where our Infant Redeemer is laid.

2 Cold on His cradle the dew-drops are shining,
  Low lies His head with the beasts of the stall;
Angels adore Him in slumber reclining,
  Maker, and Monarch, and Saviour of all.

3 Say, shall we yield Him, in costly devotion,
  Odors of Edom, and offerings divine?
Gems of the mountain, and pearls of the ocean?
  Myrrh from the forest, or gold from the mine?

4 Vainly we offer each ample oblation,
  Vainly with gifts would His favor secure;
Richer by far is the heart's adoration,
  Dearer to God are the prayers of the poor.

5 Brightest and best of the sons of the morning,
  Dawn on our darkness, and lend us Thine aid:
Star of the east, the horizon adorning,
  Guide where our Infant Redeemer is laid.

AMEN.

20.　　　　　*7s. 6s., double.*

THE wise may bring their learning,
  The rich may bring their wealth,
And some may bring their greatness,
  And some bring strength and health:
We, too, would bring our treasures,
  To offer to the King;

22

|: We have no wealth or learning— :|
|: What shall we children bring ? :|

2 We 'll bring Him hearts that love Him,
   We 'll bring Him thankful praise,
And young souls meekly striving
   To walk in holy ways.
And these shall be the treasures
   We offer to the King,
|: And these are gifts that even— :|
   |: The poorest child may bring. :|

3 We 'll bring the little duties
   We have to do each day,
We 'll try our best to please Him
   At home, at school, at play.
And better are these treasures
   To offer to our King,
|: Than richest gifts without them— :|
   |: Yet these a child may bring. :| AMEN.

21.   *S. M.*   *(Hymnal 44.)*

HOW beauteous are their feet
      Who stand on Sion's hill :
Who bring salvation on their tongues,
   And words of peace reveal !

2 How charming is their voice :
   How sweet their tidings are !

..sion, behold thy Saviour-King,
He reigns and triumphs here."

3 How happy are our ears
That hear this joyful sound,
Which kings and prophets waited for,
And sought, but never found !

4 How blessèd are our eyes
That see this heavenly light !
Prophets and kings desired it long,
But died without the sight.

5 The watchmen join their voice,
And tuneful notes employ ;
Jerusalem breaks forth in songs,
And deserts learn the joy.

6 The Lord makes bare His arm
Through all the earth abroad :
Let every nation now behold
Their Saviour and their God.   AMEN.

LENT.

22.   5s. 4s.

REST of the weary,
Joy of the sad,
Hope of the dreary,
Light of the glad ;

24

Ilome of the stranger,
   Strength to the end,
Refuge from danger,
   Saviour and Friend.

2 Pillow where lying,
   Love rests its head,
Peace of the dying,
   Life of the dead ;
Path of the lowly,
   Prize at the end,
Breath of the holy,
   Saviour and Friend.

3 When my feet stumble,
   To Thee I cry,
Crown of the humble,
   Cross of the high.
When my steps wander,
   Over me bend,
Truer and fonder,
   Saviour and Friend.

4 Ever confessing
   Thee, I will raise
Unto Thee blessing,
   Glory and praise ;
All my endeavor,
   World without end,

Thine to be ever,
　　Saviour and Friend.　　Amen.

23.　　　　　*L. M.*　　　　*(Hymnal 62.)*

O THOU, to Whose all-searching sight
　The darkness shineth as the light,
Search, prove my heart; it looks to Thee,
O burst these bonds, and set it free.

2 Wash out its stains, refine its dross,
　Nail my affections to the cross;
　Hallow each thought, let all within
　Be clean, as Thou, my Lord, art clean.

3 If in this darksome wild I stray,
　Be Thou my light, be Thou my way:
　No foes, no violence I fear,
　No harm, while Thou, my God, art near.

4 Saviour, where'er Thy steps I see,
　Dauntless, untired, I follow Thee;
　O let Thy hand support me still,
　And lead me to Thy holy hill.　　Amen.

24.　　　　　　　7s.

JESU, Who for us didst bear
　Scorn and sorrow, toil and care,
Hearken to our lowly prayer;
　　Hear us, Holy Jesu.

2 By the prayer Thou thrice didst pray
  That the cup might pass away,
  So Thou mightest still obey ;
      Hear us, Holy Jesu.

3 By the cross which Thou didst bear,
  By the cup they bade Thee share,
  Mingled gall and vinegar ;
      Hear us, Holy Jesu.

4 By the parting of Thy clothes,
  By the mocking of Thy foes,
  As they watched Thy dying woes ;
      Hear us, Holy Jesu.

5 By the piercing of Thy Side,
  By the stream of double tide,
  Blood and water, thence supplied :
      Hear us, Holy Jesu.

6 Cleansing us from outward sin,
  And from evil thoughts within,
  That we may true pureness win ;
      Save us, Holy Jesu.   AMEN

7s.

JESU, Saviour ever mild,
  Born for us a little child
Of the Virgin undefiled ;
    Hear us, O Child Jesu !

2 Jesu, Lord of life and death,
Who to her that gave Thee breath
Subject wast in Nazareth ;
    Hear us, O Child Jesu !

3 By Thy birth and childish years,
By Thy sorrows and Thy tears,
By Thy infant wants and fears ;
    Hear us, O Child Jesu !

4 From all pride and vain conceit,
From all spite and angry heat,
From all lying and deceit ;
    Deliver us, Child Jesu.

5 From all sloth and idleness,
From rejoicing at distress,
From jealousy and selfishness ;
    Deliver us, Child Jesu,

6 From disobedience, murmuring,
Thoughts in prayer-time wandering,
From each evil word and thing ;
    Deliver us, Child Jesu.

7 That we give to sin no place,
That we never quench Thy grace,
That we ever seek Thy face ;
    We beseech Thee, Jesu.

8 When shall en   the battle sore,
   When our pilgrimage is o'er,
   Grant Thy peace for evermore ;
           We beseech Thee, Jesu.   AMEN.

7s., *double.*   *(Hymnal 53.)*

SAVIOUR, when in dust, to Thee,
    Low we bow th' adoring knee ;
When, repentant, to the skies
Scarce we lift our streaming eyes ;
Oh, by all Thy pains and woe,
Suffer'd once for man below,
Bending from Thy throne on high,
Hear our solemn litany !

2 By Thy birth and early years,
   By Thy human griefs and fears,
   By Thy fasting and distress
   In the lonely wilderness ;
   By Thy victory in the hour
   Of the subtle tempter's power ;
   Jesus, look with pitying eye ;
   Hear our solemn litany.

3 By Thine hour of dark despair,
   By Thine agony of prayer,
   By the purple robe of scorn,
   By Thy wounds, Thy crown of thorn,

By Thy cross, Thy pangs and cries,
By Thy perfect sacrifice;
Jesus, look with pitying eye;
Hear our solemn litany.

4 By Thy deep expiring groan,
By the seal'd sepulchral stone,
By Thy triumph o'er the grave,
By Thy power from death to save;
Mighty God, ascended Lord,
To Thy throne in Heaven restored,
Prince and Saviour, hear our cry,
Hear our solemn litany.			AMEN.

27.			*6s. 5s., double.*			*(Hymnal* 68.*)*

CHRISTIAN ! dost thou see them,
	On the holy ground,
How the powers of darkness
	Rage thy steps around?
Christian ! up and smite them,
	Counting gain but loss;
In the strength that cometh
	By the holy cross.

2 Christian ! dost thou feel them,
	How they work within,
Striving, tempting, luring,
	Goading into sin?

Christian ! never tremble ;
  Never be down cast ;
Gird thee for the battle,
  Watch, and pray, and fast.

3 Christian ! dost thou hear them,
    How they speak thee fair ?
"Always fast and vigil ?
    Always watch and prayer ?"
Christian ! answer boldly :
  " While I breathe I pray !"
Peace shall follow battle,
  Night shall end in day.

4 *" Well I know thy trouble,*
    O my servant true ;
Thou art very weary,
    I was weary, too ;
But that toil shall make thee
    Some day all Mine own,
And the end of sorrow
    Shall be near My throne."   Amen.

PALM-SUNDAY.

7s. 6s., double.   *(Hymnal 72.)*

ALL glory, laud, and honor
  To Thee, Redeemer, King !
To Whom the lips of children
  Made sweet Hosannas ring.

Chorus.—All glory, laud, and honor
    To Thee, Redeemer, King !
    To Whom the lips of children
    Made sweet Hosannas ring.

2 Thou art the King of Israel,
    Thou David's royal son ;
Who in the Lord's name comest ;
    The King and Blessed One.—*Chorus.*

3 The people of the Hebrews
    With palms before Thee went :
Our praise, and prayer, and anthems,
    Before Thee we present.—*Chorus.*

4 To Thee, before Thy Passion,
    They sang their hymns of praise :
To Thee, now high exalted,
    Our melody we raise.—*Chorus.*

5 Thou didst accept their praises ;
    Accept the prayers we bring,
Who in all good delightest,
    Thou good and gracious King.

Chor.—All glory, laud, and honor.   Amen

29.   8s. 7s. 4.

ONCE was heard the song of children,
    By the Saviour when on earth ;

Joyful, in the sacred temple,
  Shouts of youthful praise had birth:
    ‖: And Hosannas :‖
Loud to David's Son broke forth.

2 Palms of vict'ry strewn around Him,
    Garments spread beneath His feet,
  Prophet of the Lord they crown'd Him
    In fair Salem's crowded street:
      ‖: While Hosannas :‖
From the lips of children greet.

3 Saviour, now in Heaven reigning,
    We this day Thy glory sing;
  Not with palms Thy pathway strewing,
    We would loftier tribute bring:
      ‖: Glad Hosannas :‖
To our Prophet, Priest, and King.

4 Oh! though humble is our offering,
    Deign accept our grateful lays;
  These from children once proceeding,
    Thou didst deem perfected praise:
      ‖: Now Hosannas, :‖
Saviour, Lord, to Thee we raise.   AMEN.

30.   *7s. 6s., double.*   (*Hymnal* 219.)

WHEN, His salvation bringing,
  To Zion Jesus came,
The children all stood singing,
  Hosanna to His name;
Nor did their zeal offend Him,
  But as He rode along,
He let them still attend Him,
  And smiled to hear their song.

2 The loving Lord retaineth
  His love to children still;
Though now as King He reigneth
  On Zion's heavenly hill;
We'll flock around His banner,
  Who sits upon the throne,
And cry aloud, Hosanna
  To David's royal son.

3 For should we fail proclaiming
  Our great Redeemer's praise,
The stones, our silence shaming,
  Would their Hosannas raise.
But shall we only render
  The tribute of our words?
No; while our hearts are tender,
They, too, shall be the Lord's.   AMEN.

31.

BLESSED is He that cometh in the name of
the Lord !
Joyfully let us meet Him !
Lovingly let us greet Him !
Blessed is He that cometh in the name of the
Lord !
‖: Hosanna ! Hosanna ! Hosanna in the high-
est ! :‖
Echo His wondrous praises in the sweetest ac-
cord !
Lo ! every valley ringeth,
Tidings of joy He bringeth :
Blessed is He that cometh in the name of the
Lord !

2 Blessed is He that cometh in the name of the
Lord !
Bear we the palms before Him !
Let every heart adore Him !
Blessed is He that cometh in the name of the
Lord !
‖: Hosanna ! Hosanna ! Hosanna in the high
est ! :‖
Rest to the weary-hearted He hath kindly r
stored.
Welcome Him in your sadness !
Welcome the King of Gladness !

Blessed is He that cometh in the name of the
    Lord !

3 Blessed is He that cometh in the name of the
       Honor to Him forever !   [Lord !
      Thanks unto God the Giver !
Blessed is He that cometh in the name of the
    Lord !
  ‖: Hosanna ! Hosanna ! Hosanna in the high-
    est ! :‖
Sin He hath nobly conquered by the might of
    His word !
      Little ones round Him bending,
      Greet Him with praise unending !
Blessed is He that cometh in the name of the
    Lord !   AMEN. AMEN

PASSION WEEK.

32.   *8s. 7s., double.*   *(Hymnal 76.)*

HAIL, Thou once despisèd Jesus,
  Hail, Thou Galilean King ;
Thou didst suffer to release us,
  Thou didst free salvation bring !
Hail, Thou agonizing Saviour,
  Bearer of our sin and shame ;
By Thy merit we find favour ;
  Life is given through Thy Name.

2 Paschal Lamb, by God appointed,
    All our sins were on Thee laid ;
By Almighty love anointed,
    Thou hast full atonement made.
All Thy people are forgiven,
    Through the virtue of Thy blood :
Open'd is the gate of Heaven,
    Peace is made 'twixt man and God.

3 Jesus, hail ! enthroned in glory,
    There for ever to abide ;
All the heavenly hosts adore Thee,
    Seated at Thy Father's side ;
There for sinners Thou art pleading,
    There Thou dost our place prepare ;
Ever for us interceding,
    Till in glory we appear.

4 Worship, honor, power, and blessing
    Thou art worthy to receive ;
Loudest praises, without ceasing,
    Meet it is for us to give !
Help, ye bright angelic spirits,
    Bring your sweetest, noblest lays ;
Help to sing our Saviour's merits,
    Help to chaunt Immanuel's praise. AMEN.

33.

78.

LIGHT and comfort of my soul,
    When the billows o'er me roll ;
Thou dost bid me in Thy word,
Cast my burden on the Lord.
Jesus, Saviour, once betray'd,
Sacrifice for sinners made ;
Sinful, weak, to Thee I fly,
Save, O save me, or I die !

2 Lord, my soul in tears would mourn,
All the anguish Thou hast borne ;
In the garden I would be,
Lonely watcher still with Thee.
Thou hast suffered, Thou hast bled,
Thorns have pierc'd Thy sacred head,
Jesus, while I cling to Thee,
Let Thy sorrow plead for me.

3 Mocked and scourged—condemned to die,
On the cross extended high ;
Tenant of the lonely tomb,
Mighty conqueror o'er its gloom ;
Crowned victorious ; God of love :
In Thy Father's home above,
Grant my soul a place at last,
When the storms of life are past.   AMEN.

34.   *L. M.*   *(Hymnal ‿*

WHEN I survey the wondrous cross
     On which the Prince of Glory died,
My richest gain I count but loss,
     And pour contempt on all my pride.

2 Forbid it, Lord, that I should boast,
     Save in the death of Christ, my God :
All the vain things that charm me most,
     I sacrifice them to His blood.

3 See, from His head, His hands, His feet,
     Sorrow and love flow mingled down.
Did e'er such love and sorrow meet ?
     Or thorns compose so rich a crown ?

4 Were the whole realm of nature mine,
     That were a tribute far too small ;
Love so amazing, so divine,
     Demands my soul, my life, my all. AMEN

EASTER.

35.   *8s. 7s., double.*

DAY of wonder, day of gladness,
     Hail thy ever glorious light !
Gone is sorrow, gone is sadness,
     Ended is the gloomy night !
Listen to the angel's story,
     Cast away all doubt and dread ;

Give to God, the Father, glory,
  " Christ is risen from the dead !"

2 In the triumph of this hour,
  Jubilant shall swell the song ;
Unto Jesus honor, power,
  Blessing, victory belong.
Scattered are the clouds of error,
  Sin and hell are captive led,
E'en the grave is freed from terror,
  " Christ is risen from the dead !"

3 Every people, every nation
  Soon shall hear the gladsome sound,
Joyous tidings of salvation
  Borne to earth's remotest bound.
Then shall rise in tones excelling,
  Praise for grace so freely shed,
And the Easter hymn be swelling,
  " Christ is risen from the dead !"

4 Victor now, to heaven ascended,
  Seated on the Father's throne,
Christ, in whom our nature blended,
  Will His blessed children own,
If above in glory meeting,
  We the heavenly courts should tread,
Sweeter then will sound the greeting,
  " Christ is risen from the dead !" AMEN

36.   7s. 8s.   *(Hymnal 104.)*

JESUS lives! no longer now
   Can thy terrors, Death, appal us:
Jesus lives! by this we know
   Thou, O Grave, canst not enthrall us.
                  Alleluia!

2 Jesus lives! henceforth is death
   But the gate of life immortal;
This shall calm our trembling breath,
   When we pass its gloomy portal.
                  Alleluia!

3 Jesus lives! for us He died:
   Then alone to Jesus living,
Pure in heart may we abide,
   Glory to our Saviour giving.
                  Alleluia!

4 Jesus lives! our hearts know well
   Nought from us His love shall sever;
Life, nor death, nor powers of hell
   Tear us from His keeping ever,
                  Alleluia!

5 Jesus lives! to Him the throne
   Over all the world is given:
May we go where He is gone,
   Rest and reign with Him in Heaven.
                  Alleluia!   AMEN.

37.

PUT on, put on your best array,
  Let us make glad holiday ;
  Merrily the church bells ring,
  Cheerily the angels sing,
Christ the Lord is risen to-day,
  This Easter day.

2 Sing, sing ye birds on ev'ry tree,
  Carol, warblers o'er the lea ;
  Gone are winter's gloomy days,
  Banished by the sun's bright rays ;
Christ from death hath set us free,
  This Easter day.

3 Spring, spring, ye flowers of richest dyes,
  Lift to heaven your dewy eyes ;
  Spring has come from God on high,
  We wake to life, no more to die,
Christ the Risen bids us rise
  This Easter day.

4 Depart, depart, ye shades of night,
  Before our Risen Sun's great light ;
  Lift we up our chant of praise,
  Quickened by His orient rays,
All is glorious, all is bright
  This Easter day.   AMEN.

38. 7s. *(Hymnal 98.)*

CHRIST the Lord is risen to-day; Alleluia!
  Sons of men, and angels say; Alleluia!
Raise your joys and triumphs high; Alleluia!
Sing, ye heavens, and earth reply; Alleluia!

2 Love's redeeming work is done; Alleluia!
Fought the fight, the victory won; Alleluia!
Jesus' agony is o'er; Alleluia!
Darkness veils the earth no more; Alleluia!

3 Vain the stone, the watch, the seal; Alleluia!
Christ hath burst the gates of hell; Alleluia!
Death in vain forbids Him rise; Alleluia!
Christ hath opened Paradise; Alleluia!

4 Soar we now where Christ hath led; Alleluia!
Following our exalted Head; Alleluia!
Made like Him, like Him we rise; Alleluia!
Ours the cross, the grave, the skies; Alleluia!
AMEN.

39

CHRIST hath arisen!
  Death is no more!
Lo! the white-robed ones
  Sit by the door.
||: Dawn, golden morning,
  Scatter the night!

Haste, ye disciples glad,
   First with the light. :‖

2 Break forth in singing,
   O world, new-born !
Chaunt the great Easter-tide,
   Christ's holy morn.
‖: Chaunt Him, young sunbeams,
   Dancing in mirth !
Chaunt, all ye winds of God,
   Coursing the earth ! :‖

3 Chaunt Him, ye laughing flowers,
   Fresh from the sod :
Chaunt Him, wild leaping streams,
   Praising your God !
‖: Break from thy winter
   Sad heart, and sing !
Bud with thy blossoms fair ;
   Christ is thy spring. :‖

4 Come where the Lord hath lain,
   Past is the gloom ;
See the full eye of day
   Smile through the tomb.
‖: Hark ! angel voices
   Fall from the skies !
Christ hath arisen !
   Glad heart arise ! :‖   AMEN.

40.
8s. 6s., double.

HOW in the flow'ry spring, my God,
  The buds of promise ope,
And blossom o'er life's thorny road,
  To cheer the Christian's hope!
Like them, exulting from the tomb,
  We, too, revived, shall rise
And flourish in immortal bloom,
  ‖: In Edens of the skies :‖

2 What though in pensive autumn's wane,
  Earth's sere grown glories fall,
And sleep through winter's dull domain,
  When death is writ on all.
Exulting in the breaking year,
  The lily doth unclose,
And daisies o'er the waste appear,
  ‖: And roses from the snows. :‖

3 So then to dust, our dust shall turn,
  So too shall rise and sing,
When falls upon the mouldered urn
  The joyous dew of spring ;
The God that rears the tender flowers,
  And breathes to life their dust,
From the cold grave shall quicken ours,
  ‖: And new-create the just. :‖   AMEN.

41.

" HE is risen, He is not here;
    Seek Him not among the dead;
He is living, do not fear,"
So the white-robed angel said.
He hath conquer'd ev'ry foe,
He hath shown His power to save,
When He took the sting from death
And the vict'ry from the grave.

Chorus.—Then with one heart and voice
    Let all the earth rejoice;
    Let all the living join the strain,
    And angels shout it back again:
    The Lord is risen, the Lord is risen
    Rejoice, rejoice, rejoice, rejoice!

2 He is risen, He is not here;
On the earth He walks no more;
All His trials, all His toils,
All His griefs and shame are o'er,
All His purpose is fulfilled,
All His work on earth is done:
He Whom sinners put to death
Sitteth on the great white throne.—*Chor.*

3 He is risen, He is not here—
Not indeed to mortal eyes;

But we all who die with Him,
Shall again with Him arise.
'T is in Him alone we live.
And because He lives again—
Blessed promise, glorious hope !
We shall with Him live and reign.—*Chor.*

Amen.

42.

CHILDREN, come and we 'll sing the wonder-
    ful love
Of Him who came from bright Heaven above;
Light from the grave illumes the sky,
For Jesus hath triumphed and reigns on high.

Chorus.—Now in Easter's glad tide, join with
    loud acclaim,
        To Christ, our dear Saviour ; praise ye
        His holy Name.

2 When for three weary days He lay in the tomb,
The earth was shrouded in darkest gloom ;
But now let praises fill the sky,
For Christ has arisen, and now reigns on
high.—*Chor.*

3 A bright angel came down from Heaven above,
The heavy stone from the tomb to move ;
Jesus came forth, no more to die,
For He has arisen, and reigns on high.—*Chor.*

4 He has conquered for ever death and the grave,
And He is mighty and waits to save;
Fly, then, to Him for refuge, fly;
For Christ has arisen, and reigns on high.—

Chor. AMEN.

43.

CHRIST is risen! Christ is risen!
Glory to the Father's Name!
Christ is risen! Christ is risen!
Go the joyful news,
The joyful news proclaim!
Go, the joyful news proclaim!

Solo.—Death forever He hath conquer'd,
And He reigneth now on high!
Christ is risen! Christ is risen!
God the Saviour glorify.

Chorus.—Shout Hosanna! He is Victor
O'er the terrors of the grave!
Christ is risen! Christ is risen!
All His children He will save!

2 All ye nations bow before Him,
He is God forevermore!
With the Father now He reigneth,
Heaven and earth His Name,
His holy Name adore,
Heaven and earth His Name adore.

Solo.—He hath opened to His people
Heaven's gates eternally !
Christ is risen ! Christ is risen !
Spread the news from sea to sea !
Chor.—Shout Hosanna ! He is Victor, etc. AMEN

44.

CHRIST is risen ! Christ is risen !
Christ the Lord is ris'n to-day ;
Christ is risen ! Christ is risen !
Sons of men and angels say.

Semi-chor.—May each face with gladness glisten
Let not one refuse His praise :
Let no tears our eyelids moisten,
While our voices high we raise.

Chorus.—For Christ is risen ! Christ is risen !
That he who dies with Him may rise.

Solo.—Love's redeeming work is done,
Fought the fight, the vict'ry won :
Jesus' agony is o'er,
Darkness veils the earth no more.

Chor.—For Christ is risen ! etc.

2 Christ is risen ! Christ is risen !
Raise your joys and triumphs high ;
Christ is risen ! Christ is risen !
Sing, ye heavens, and earth reply.

Semi-chor.—May our hearts, with love o'erflowing,
Grateful off'rings to Him bring;
Off'rings of our heart's devotion
To our Saviour, Christ, our King.
Chor.—For Christ is risen! etc.
Solo.—Soar we now where Christ hath led,
Following our exalted Head;
Made like Him, like Him we rise:
Ours the cross, the grave, the skies.
Chor.—For Christ is risen! etc.   AMEN.

45.

WHO is He in yonder stall
At Whose feet the shepherds fall?
Chorus.—'Tis the Lord, O wondrous story!
'T is the Lord, the King of glory,
At His feet we humbly fall,
Crown Him, crown Him, Lord of all!

2 Who is He in yonder cot
Bending to His toilsome lot?—*Chor.*

3 Who is He Who stands and weeps,
At the grave where Lazarus sleeps?—*Chor.*

4 Who is He in deep distress,
Fasting in the wilderness?—*Chor.*

5 Lo! at midnight Who is He,
Prays in dark Gethsemane?—*Chor.*

6 Who is He in Calvary's throes,
   Asks for blessings on His foes ?—*Chor.*

7 Who is He that from the grave,
   Comes to heal, and help, and save ?—*Chor.*

8 Who is He that on yon throne,
   Rules the world of light alone ?—*Chor.*

AMEN

ASCENSION.

46.   *8s. 7s., double.*

SEE the Conqueror mounts in triumph,
   See the King in royal state
Riding on, the clouds His chariot,
   To His Heavenly palace gate :
Hark ! the choirs of angel voices
   Joyful Alleluias sing ;
And the portals high are lifted
   To receive their Heavenly King.

2 Who is this that comes in glory,
   With the trump of jubilee ?
Lord of battles, God of armies,
   He has gained the victory :
He Who on the cross did suffer,
   He Who from the grave arose ;
He has vanquished sin and Satan,
   He by death has spoiled His foes.

51

3 While He lifts His hands in blessing,
     He is parted from His friends ;
  While their eager eyes behold Him,
     He upon the clouds ascends.
  He has raised our human nature
     In the clouds to God's right hand ;
  There we sit in heavenly places,
     There with Him in glory stand.   Amen.

47.   8s. 7s. 4.   *(Hymnal 115.)*

LOOK, ye saints ; the sight is glorious ;
     See the " Man of sorrows " now ;
  From the fight returned victorious,
     Every knee to Him shall bow ;
        Crown Him !   Crown Him !
  Crowns become the Victor's brow.

2 Crown the Saviour, angels crown Him ;
     Rich the trophies Jesus brings ;
  On the seat of power enthrone Him,
     While the vault of heaven rings !
        Crown Him !   Crown Him !
  Crown the Saviour King of kings !

3 Sinners in derision crowned Him,
     Mocking thus the Saviour's claim ;
  Saints and angels crowd around Him,
     Own His title, praise His Name ;

Crown Him!   Crown Him!
Spread abroad the Victor's fame!

4 Hark! those bursts of acclamation!
   Hark! those loud triumphant chords!
Jesus takes the highest station;
   O what joy the sight affords!
      Crown Him!   Crown Him!
King of kings, and Lord of lords!   Amen.

48.   *L. M.*   *(Hymnal 117.)*

OUR Lord is risen from the dead,
   Our Jesus is gone up on high;
The powers of hell are captive led,
   Dragg'd to the portals of the sky.

2 There His triumphal chariot waits,
   And angels chant the solemn lay:
" *Lift up your heads, ye heavenly gates,*
   Ye everlasting doors, give way.'

3 Loose all your bars of massy light,
   And wide unfold the radiant scene;
He claims those mansions as His right;
   Receive the King of Glory in.

4 " *Who is the King of Glory, who?* "
   The Lord that all His foes o'ercame,
The world, sin, death, and hell o'erthrew;
   And Jesus is the conqueror's Name.

5 Lo ! His triumphal chariot waits,
    And angels chant the solemn lay ;
 " *Lift up your heads, ye heavenly gates,*
    Ye everlasting doors, give way."

6 " *Who is the King of Glory, who ?*"
    The Lord, of boundless power possess'd,
 The King of saints and angels, too,
    God over all, for ever bless'd.   AMEN.

WHITSUNTIDE.

49.   *C. M.*   *(Hymnal 125.)*

HE'S come ! let every knee be bent,
    All hearts new joy resume ;
 Sing, ye redeem'd, with one consent,
    " The Comforter is come."

2 What greater gift, what greater love,
    Could God on man bestow ?
 Angels for this rejoice above,
    Let man rejoice below.

3 Hail, blessed Spirit ! may each soul
    Thy sacred influence feel ;
 Do Thou each sinful thought control,
    And fix our wavering zeal.

4 Thou to the conscience dost convey
    Those checks which we should know ;

Thy motions point to us the way ;
   Thou giv'st us strength to go.   AMEN.

50.   *C. M.*   *(Hymnal* 128.*)*

COME, Holy Spirit, Heavenly Dove,
   With all Thy quickening powers,
Kindle a flame of sacred love
   In these cold hearts of ours.

2 See how we grovel here below,
   Fond of these earthly toys :
Our souls, how heavily they go,
   To reach eternal joys.

3 In vain we tune our lifeless songs,
   In vain we strive to rise :
Hosannas languish on our tongues,
   And our devotion dies.

4 Come, Holy Spirit, Heavenly Dove,
   With all Thy quickening powers,
Come, shed abroad a Saviour's love,
   And that shall kindle ours.   AMEN.

51.   *L. M.*   *(Hymnal* 126.*)*

O SPIRIT of the living God,
   In all Thy plenitude of grace,
Where'er the foot of man hath trod,
   Descend on our apostate race.

2 Give tongues of fire and hearts of love,
   To preach the reconciling word ;
Give power and unction from above,
   Where'er the joyful sound is heard.

3 Be darkness, at Thy coming, light ;
   Confusion, order, in Thy path ;
Souls without strength inspire with might ;
   Bid mercy triumph over wrath.

4 Convert the nations ; far and nigh
   The triumphs of the cross record ;
The Name of Jesus glorify,
   Till every people call Him Lord.   AMEN.

TRINITY SUNDAY.

52.   *(Hymnal 138.)*

HOLY, holy, holy ! Lord God Almighty !
   Early in the morning our song shall rise
      to Thee :
Holy, holy, holy ! merciful and mighty !
God in Three Persons, Blessed Trinity !

2 Holy, holy, holy ! all the saints adore Thee,
Casting down their golden crowns around the
      glassy sea ;   [Thee,
Cherubim and seraphim falling down before
Which wert, and art, and evermore shall be.

3 Holy, holy, holy! though the darkness hide
      Thee,
  Though the eye of sinful man Thy glory may
      not see;
  Only Thou art holy; there is none beside Thee
  Perfect in power, in love, and purity.

4 Holy, holy, holy! Lord God Almighty!
  All Thy works shall praise Thy Name, in earth,
      and sky, and sea:
  Holy, holy, holy! merciful and mighty;
  God in Three Persons, Blessed Trinity!

AMEN.

53. 7s.

HOLY Father! hear my cry;
    Holy Saviour! bend Thine ear;
  Holy Spirit! come Thou nigh;
    Father, Saviour, Spirit, hear.

2 Father, save me from my sin;
    Saviour, I Thy mercy crave;
  Gracious Spirit! make me clean;
    Father, Son, and Spirit, save.

3 Father, let me taste Thy love;
    Saviour, fill my soul with peace;
  Spirit, come my heart to move;
    Father, Son, and Spirit, bless.

4 Father, Son, and Spirit—Thou
  One Jehovah, shed abroad
All Thy grace within me now;
  Be my Father and my God.   AMEN.

54.   6s. 4s.   *(Hymnal 428.)*

COME, Thou Almighty King,
  Help us Thy Name to sing,
    Help us to praise !
Father, all glorious,
O'er all victorious,
Come and reign over us,
    Ancient of days.

2 Come, Thou Incarnate Word,
  Gird on Thy mighty sword ;
    Our prayer attend !
Come, and Thy people bless :
Come, give Thy word success ;
Spirit of holiness,
    On us descend !

3 Come, Holy Comforter,
  Thy sacred witness bear,
    In this glad hour :
Thou, Who Almighty art,
Now rule in every heart,
And ne'er from us depart ;
    Spirit of Power.

4 To Thee, great One in Three,
   The highest praises be,
     Hence evermore ;
   Thy sovereign majesty
   May we in glory see,
   And to eternity
     Love and adore.   Amen

55.   6s. 8s.   *(Hymnal 143.)*

WE give immortal praise
   To God the Father's love,
For all our comforts here,
   And all our hopes above :
He sent His own Eternal Son
To die for sins that man had done.

2   To God the Son belongs
     Immortal glory, too,
   Who saved us by His blood
     From everlasting woe :
And now He lives, and now He reigns,
And sees the fruit of all His pains.

3   To God the Spirit's Name
     Immortal worship give,
   Whose new-creating power
     Makes the dead sinner live :
His work completes the great design,
And fills the soul with joy divine.

4   Almighty God, to Thee
     Be endless honors done ;
    The undivided Three,
     And the mysterious One ;
 Where reason fails with all her powers,
 There faith prevails and love adores. AMEN.

56   *7s., with chorus.* *(Hymnal* 220.*)*

GLORY to the Father give,
  God in Whom we move and live ;
 Children's prayers He deigns to hear,
 Children's songs delight His ear.

Chorus.—Hallelujah ! Hallelujah ! Hallelujah !
          AMEN.

2 Glory to the Son we bring,
 Christ our Prophet, Priest, and King ;
 Children, raise your sweetest strain
 To the Lamb, for He was slain.—*Chor.*

3 Glory to the Holy Ghost,
 He reclaims the sinner lost ;
 Children's minds may He inspire,
 Touch their tongues with holy fire.—*Chor.*

4 Glory in the highest be
 To the blessed Trinity,
 For the Gospel from above,
 For the word that " God is love."—*Chor.*
        AMEN.

THE LORD'S DAY.

57.   7s.   *(Hymnal 163.)*

TO Thy temple I repair ;
    Lord, I love to worship there ;
While Thy glorious praise is sung,
Touch my lips, unloose my tongue.

2 While the prayers of saints ascend,
    God of love, to mine attend ;
Hear me, for Thy Spirit pleads ;
Hear, for Jesus intercedes.

3 While I hearken to Thy law,
    Fill my soul with humble awe ;
Till Thy Gospel bring to me
Life and immortality.

4 While Thy ministers proclaim
    Peace and pardon in Thy Name.
Through their voice, by faith, may I
Hear Thee speaking from on high.

5 From Thy house when I return,
    May my heart within me burn ;
And at evening let me say,
" I have walked with God to-day."   AMEN.

58.

SWEET the Sabbath morning,
    Calm and bright returning,

Seems to subdue the turmoil of the week ;
    Sabbath bells inviting,
    Children all uniting,
Sweetly sing the praise of Him, Whose throne
    Jesus is near them,   [they seek.
    Jesus will hear them,
Yes, He will hear those sweet notes they raise.
    Every Sabbath morning
    See their footsteps turning,
Where they learn to sing and speak a Sav-
    iour's praise.

2   Sweetest day of seven ;
    Pointing us to Heaven ;
Thou beacon-light upon life's stormy sea !
    Rest we from our labor ;
    Sharing with our neighbor
All the holy peace and joy that comes with
    Sweet Sabbath morning,   [Thee.
    Blessed thy returning ;
Oh ! may we treasure these Sabbath days !
    Hark ! a voice is calling ;
    Through the stillness falling ;
Calling us to meet and sing our Saviour's
    praise.

3   Every Sabbath morning
    Sinful pleasure scorning,

Our Sunday-school shall be a sacred spot;
   There our voices ringing,
   With the angels singing,
Lead our thoughts away where care and sin
   Oh ! holy pleasure,   [are not.
   Oh ! heavenly treasure,
We'll ever prize these sweet Sabbath days !
   Bringing Heaven nearer; ·
   Making Jesus dearer ;
Fitting us to join His saints, and see His face.
                           Amen.

59.   7s. 6s., *double.*   (*Hymnal* 160.)

O DAY of rest and gladness,
   O day of joy and light,
O balm of care and sadness,
   Most beautiful, most bright ;
On thee, the high and lowly,
   Through ages join'd in tune,
Sing, Holy, holy, holy,
   To the Great God Triune.

2 On thee, at the creation,
   The light first had its birth ;
On thee, for our salvation,
   Christ rose from depths of earth ;
On thee, our Lord victorious
   The spirit sent from Heaven,

And thus on thee, most glorious,
  A triple light was given.

3 To-day on weary nations
  The heavenly manna falls :
In holy convocations,
  The silver trumpet calls,
Where gospel-light is glowing
  With pure and radiant beams :
The living water flowing
  With soul-refreshing streams.

4 New graces ever gaining
  From this our day of rest,
We reach the rest remaining
  To spirits of the blest ;
To Holy Ghost be praises,
  To Father, and to Son ;
The Church her voice upraises
  To Thee blest Three in One.   AMEN.

II.—CREATION.

60.   *7s. 6s., double.*

THE fields bedecked with flowers,
  The stars that gem the night,
The sunbeams and the showers,
  God made them in His might.

CREATION.

Each little flower that opens,
  Each little bird that sings,
He made their glowing colors,
  He made their tiny wings.

2 The rich man in his castle,
  The poor man at his gate,
He made them high or lowly,
  And ordered their estate.
The purple-headed mountains,
  The river running by,
The sunset and the morning
  That lightens up the sky;

3 The cold winds in the winter,
  The pleasant summer sun,
The ripe fruits in the garden,
  He made them, every one.
The tall trees in the greenwood,
  The meadows where we play,
The rushes by the water
  We gather every day;

4 He gave us eyes to see them,
  And lips that we might tell,
How great is God Almighty,
  Who " doeth all things well."
Then let us raise our voices
  His praises to proclaim,
And in His works around us,
  Read His almighty Name.   Amen,

61.   *(Hymnal 425.)*

THE strain upraise of joy and *praise*, Alle- |
    luia !
To the glory of their King
Shall the *ran*som'd | people sing, ‖ *Al*le- | lu-
    ia ! ‖ *Al*le | luia !
And the *choirs* that | dwell on high,
Shall re-*echo* | through the sky, ‖ *Al*le- | luia ! ‖
    *Al*le- | luia !

2 They in the *rest* of | Paradise who dwell,
The blessed ones with *joy* the | chorus swell, ‖
    *Al*le- | luia ! ‖ *Al*le | luia !
The planets beaming *on* their | heavenly way,
The shining constella*tions*, | join and say, ‖
    *Al*le- | luia ! ‖ *Al*le- | luia !

3   Ye clouds that onward sweep,
        Ye *winds* on | pinions light,
    Ye thunders, echoing loud and deep,
        Ye light*nings*, | wildly bright,
    In *sweet* con- | sent unite ‖ *your* Alle- | luia !

4   Ye floods and ocean billows,
        Ye *storms* and | winter snow,
    Ye days of cloudless beauty,
        Hoar *frost* and | summer glow :
    Ye groves that wave in spring,
    And *glo*rious | forests, sing, ‖ *Al*le- | luia !

5 First let the birds, with *paint*ed | plumage gay,
Exalt their great Crea*tor's* | praise, and say,
    *Al*le- | luia ! ‖ *Al*le- | luia !

Then let the beasts of *earth*, with | varying
  strain,
Join in creation's *hymn* and | cry again, | *Alle-*
  | luia ! | *Alle-* | luia !

6 Here let the mountains thunder *forth* so- | nor-
  ous, | *Alle-* | luia !
There let the valleys sing in *gentle*r | chorus, |
  Alle | luia !
Thou jubilant *abyss* of | ocean, cry, | *Alle-* |
  luia !
Ye tracts of earth and *conti-* | nents, reply |
  Alle- | luia !

7 To God, who *all* cre- | ation made,
The frequent *hymn* be | duly paid : | *Alle·* |
  luia ! | *Alle-* | luia !
This is the strain, the eternal strain, the *Lord*
  Al- | mighty loves : | *Alle-* | luia !
This is the song, the heavenly song, that *Christ*,
  the | King, approves : | *Alle-* | luia !
Wherefore we sing, both heart and *voice* a- |
  waking, | *Alle-* | luia !
And children's voices echo, an*swer* | making, |
  Alle- | luia !

8   Now from all *men* | be outpoured
    Allelu*ia* | to the Lord ;—
    With Allelu*ia* | evermore
    The Son and Spir*it* | we adore.
    Praise be *done* to the | Three in One.
      Alle | luia ! | *Alle-* | luia ! | *Alle—*luia ! |
                AMEN.

62.   5s. 6s. 5.   *(Hymnal 519.)*

O WORSHIP the King,
    All glorious above ;
O gratefully sing
    His power and His love ;
Our Shield and Defender,
    The Ancient of days,
Pavilion'd in splendor,
    And girded with praise.

2 O tell of His might,
    O sing of His grace,
Whose robe is the light ;
    Whose canopy, space.
His chariots of wrath
    Deep thunder-clouds form,
And dark is His path
    On the wings of the storm.

3 The earth, with its store,
    Of wonders untold,
Almighty, Thy power
    Hath founded of old—
Hath stablished it fast
    By a changeless decree,
And round it hath cast,
    Like a mantle, the sea.

4 Thy bountiful care
    What tongue can recite ?
It breathes in the air,
    It shines in the light ;
It streams from the hills ;
    It descends to the plain,
And sweetly distils
    In the dew and the rain.

5 Frail children of dust,
    And feeble as frail,
In Thee do we trust,
    Nor find Thee to fail.
Thy mercies, how tender,
    How firm to the end ;
Our Maker, Defender,
    Redeemer, and Friend !

6 O measureless might,
    Ineffable Love !
While angels delight
    To hymn Thee above,
The humbler creation,
    Though feeble their lays,
With true adoration
    Shall lisp to Thy praise.   AMEN

III.—PROVIDENCE.

63. *Six 8s.* *(Hymnal 504.)*

THE Lord my pasture shall prepare,
  And feed me with a shepherd's care ;
His presence shall my wants supply,
And guard me with a watchful eye :
My noonday walks He shall attend,
And all my midnight hours defend.

2 When in the sultry glebe I faint,
Or on the thirsty mountain pant,
To fertile vales and dewy meads,
My weary, wand'ring steps He leads,
Where peaceful rivers, soft and slow,
Amid the verdant landscape flow.

3 Though in the paths of death I tread,
With gloomy horrors overspread,
My steadfast heart shall fear no ill,
For Thou, O Lord ! art with me still ;
Thy friendly crook shall give me aid,
And guide me through the dismal shade.

AMEN.

64.

HE leadeth me ! O blessed thought !
  O words with heavenly comfort fraught !

Whate'er I do, where'er I be,
Still 't is God's hand that leadeth me!

Chorus.—He leadeth me! He leadeth me!
By His own hand He leadeth me;
His faithful follower I would be,
For by His hand He leadeth me.

2 Sometimes 'mid scenes of deepest gloom,
Sometimes where Eden's bowers bloom,
By waters still, o'er troubled sea—
Still 't is His hand that leadeth me.—*Chor.*

3 Lord, I would clasp Thy hand in mine,
Nor ever murmur nor repine—
Content whatever lot I see,
Since 't is my God that leadeth me.—*Chor.*

4 And when my task on earth is done,
When, by Thy grace, the victory's won,
E'en death's cold wave I will not flee,
Since God through Jordan leadeth me.—*Chor.*

AMEN.

65.   8s. 7s.   *(Hymnal 469.)*

GOD shall charge His angel legions,
Watch and ward o'er thee to keep;
Though thou walk through hostile regions,
Though in desert wilds thou sleep.

2 On the lion vainly roaring,
    On his young, thy foot shall tread;
And, the dragon's den exploring,
    Thou shalt bruise the serpent's head.

3 Since, with pure and firm affection,
    Thou on God hast set thy love,
With the wings of His protection
    He will shield thee from above.

4 Thou shalt call on Him in trouble,
    He will hearken, He will save;
Here for grief reward thee double,
    Crown with life beyond the grave.   AMEN.

66.   *8s. 7s. 4.*   *(Hymnal 505.)*

GUIDE me, O Thou great Jehovah,
    Pilgrim through this barren land;
I am weak, but Thou art mighty:
    Hold me with Thy powerful hand:
        ‖: Bread of heaven, :‖
Feed me now and evermore.

2 Open now the crystal fountain,
    Whence the healing streams do flow;
Let the fiery cloudy pillar
    Lead me all my journey through:
        ‖: Strong Deliverer :‖
Be Thou still my Strength and Shield.

3 When I tread the verge of Jordan,
  Bid my anxious fears subside,
Death of death and hell's destruction,
  Land me safe on Canaan's side:
    ‖: Songs of praises :‖
  I will ever give to Thee.   AMEN.

67.   *C. M.*   *(Hymnal 326.)*

GOD of our fathers, by Whose hand
    Thy people still are blest,
Be with us through our pilgrimage ;
  Conduct us to our rest.

2 Through each perplexing path of life
    Our wandering footsteps guide ;
Give us each day our daily bread,
    And raiment fit provide.

3 O spread Thy sheltering wings around,
    Till all our wanderings cease,
And, at our Father's loved abode
    Our souls arrive in peace.

4 Such blessings from Thy gracious hand
    Our humble prayers implore ;
And Thou, the Lord, shalt be our God,
    And 'portion evermore.   AMEN.

68.   *C. M.*   *(Hymnal 415.)*

THROUGH all the changing scenes of life,
    In trouble or in joy,
The praises of my God shall still
    My heart and tongue employ.

2 The angel of the Lord encamps
    Around the good and just;
Deliv'rance He affords to all
    Who on His succor trust.

3 O make but trial of His love,
    Experience will decide
How blest they are, and only they,
    Who in His truth confide.

4 Fear Him, ye saints; and you will then
    Have nothing else to fear;
Make you His service your delight,
    Your wants shall be His care.   AMEN.

69.

THRO' the day so rosy bright,
    Thro' the darkness of the night,
What tho' dim may be our sight,
        He leads us on!
Over rough, untrodden ways,
Thro' the world's bewild'ring maze,
He is with us all our days,—
        He leads us on!

Chorus.—Yes, our Father leads us on,
   Till the work of life is done !
   On His breast, in love we rest,—
    He leads us on !

2 Bowed beneath His heavenly will,
May His love our bosoms fill !
By the waters, cool and still,
   He leads us on !
Leaning on His mighty arm,
Pain and death no more alarm ;
Safe from woes, and safe from harm
   He leads us on !—*Chor.*

IV.—REDEMPTION.

70.   8s. 7s. 4.

JESUS is our loving Saviour !
 He, our best, and constant friend ;
In His service life is pleasure,
 For He loveth to the end.
  ‖: Loving Saviour ! :‖
Here we at Thy footstool bend.

2 Jesus is the children's Saviour !
 'Twas for them He shed His blood ;
Died, that poor and needy sinners
 Might be reconciled to God.
  ‖: Dying Saviour ! :‖
Bearing thus our sinful load.

3 Jesus is the children's Saviour !
  " Suffer them," He says, " to come,"
If they seek His face and favor,
  They shall share His heavenly home.
    ‖: Risen Saviour ! :‖
Never more from Thee to roam.

4 Loving, suffering, dying Saviour !
  Risen, glorious on Thy throne !
Haste the day when every idol
  Shall by truth be overthrown.
    ‖: And the kingdoms :‖
Of the earth, To thee belong.   Amen.

71.   *C. M., with chorus.*   *(Hymnal 369.)*

SALVATION, O the joyful sound !
  Glad tidings to our ears ;
A sovereign balm for every wound,
  A cordial for our fears.
Chorus.—Glory, honor, praise, and power,
      Be unto the Lamb forever !
      Jesus Christ is our Redeemer !
      Hallelujah ! Hallelujah !
      Hallelujah ! praise the Lord.

2 Buried in sorrow and in sin,
  At hell's dark door we lay,
But we arise by grace divine,
  To see a heavenly day.—*Chor.*

3 Salvation ! let the echo fly
      The spacious earth around ;
  While all the armies of the sky
      Conspire to raise the sound.—*Chor.*

AMEN.

72.   *C. M.*   *(Hymnal 372.)*
  TO our Redeemer's glorious Name
      Awake the sacred song ;
  O may His love (immortal flame !)
      Tune every heart and tongue.

2 His love, what mortal thought can reach,
      What mortal tongue display !
  Imaginations' utmost stretch
      In wonder dies away.

3 He left His radiant throne on high,
      Left the bright realms of bliss,
  And came to earth to bleed and die :
      Was ever love like this ?

4 Dear Lord, while we adoring pay
      Our humble thanks to Thee,
  May every heart with rapture say,
      " The Saviour died for me."

5 O may the sweet, the blissful theme,
      Fill every heart and tongue ;
  Till strangers love Thy charming Name,
      And join the sacred song.   AMEN.

73. *C. M.* *(Hymnal 396.)*

FOR ever here my rest shall be
Close to Thy bleeding side ;
This all my hope and all my plea,
" For me the Saviour died."

2 My dying Saviour and my God,
Fountain for guilt and sin !
Sprinkle me ever with Thy blood,
And cleanse and keep me clean.

3 Wash me, and make me thus thine own ;
Wash me, and mine Thou art ;
Wash me, but not my feet alone—
My hands, my head, my heart.

4 The atonement of Thy blood apply,
Till faith to sight improve ;
Till hope in full fruition die,
And all my soul is love.   AMEN.

74. *(Hymnal 384.)*

THE voice of free grace
Cries, Escape to the mountain ;
For Adam's lost race
Christ hath opened a fountain ;
For sin and uncleanness
And every transgression,
His blood flows most freely
In streams of salvation.

Chorus.—Hallelujah to the Lamb
        Who hath bought us our pardon ;
        ‖: We 'll praise Him again
        When we pass over Jordan. :‖

2 Ye souls that are wounded,
     To Jesus repair !
   He calls you in mercy,
     And can you forbear ?
   Though your sins be as scarlet,
     Still flee to the mountain ;
   That blood can remove them
     Which streams from this fountain.— *Chor.*

3 O Jesus ! ride onward,
     Triumphantly glorious ;
   O'er sin, death, and hell
     Thou 'rt more than victorious ;
   Thy Name is the theme
     Of the great congregation,
   While angels and saints
     Raise the shout of salvation.—*Chor*

4 With joy shall we stand
     When escaped to that shore ;
   With our harps in our hand
     We will praise Him the more :
   We 'll range the sweet fields
     On the banks of the river

And sing of salvation
For ever and ever.—*Chor.*   AMEN.

75.   6*s.* 8*s.*

BLOW ye the trumpet, blow
    The gladly solemn sound !
Let all the nations know,
    To earth's remotest bound,
The year of jubilee is come !
Return, ye ransom'd sinners, home.

2   Exalt the Lamb of God,
        The sin-atoning Lamb !
    Redemption by His blood
        Through all the lands proclaim :
    The year of jubilee is come !
    Return, ye ransom'd sinners, home.

3   The gospel trumpet hear,
        The news of pardoning grace,
    Ye happy souls, draw near,
        Behold your Saviour's face ;
    The year of jubilee is come !
    Return, ye ransom'd sinners, home.

4   Jesus, our great High-Priest,
        Has full atonement made ;
    Ye weary spirits, rest,
        Ye mournful souls, be glad ;

The year of jubilee is come!
Return, ye ransom'd sinners, home.   Amen

V.—THE SCRIPTURES.

76.   *7s. 6s., double.*   *(Hymnal 362.)*

O WORD of God Incarnate,
  O Wisdom from on high,
O Truth unchanged, unchanging,
  O Light of our dark sky!
We praise Thee for the radiance
  That from the hallow'd page,
A lantern to our footsteps,
  Shines on from age to age.

2 The Church from her dear Master
    Received the gift divine,
  And still that light she lifteth
    O'er all the earth to shine.
  It is the golden casket
    Where gems of truth are stored;
  It is the heaven-drawn picture
    Of Christ the living Word.

3 It floateth like a banner
    Before God's host unfurl'd;
  It shineth like a beacon
    Above the darkling world;

It is the chart and compass
  That o'er life's surging sea,
Mid mists, and rocks, and quicksands,
  Still guide, O Christ, to Thee.

4 O make Thy Church, dear Saviour,
  A lamp of burnish'd gold,
To bear before the nations
  Thy true light as of old ;
O teach Thy wandering pilgrims
  By this their path to trace,
Till, clouds and darkness ended,
  They see Thee face to face.   AMEN.

77.   11s.

THE Bible ! the Bible ! more precious than
    gold
The hopes and the glories its pages unfold ;
It speaks of a Saviour and tells of His love ;
‖: It shows us the way to the mansions above. :‖

2 The Bible ! the Bible ! blest volume of truth,
How sweetly it smiles on the season of youth !
It bids us seek early the pearl of great price,
‖: Ere the heart is enslaved in the bondage of
    vice. :‖

3 The Bible ! the Bible ! we hail it with joy,
Its truths and its glories our tongue shall em-
    ploy .

We 'll sing of its triumphs, we 'll tell of its
worth,
|: And send its glad tidings afar o'er the earth. :|
AMEN.

VI.—THE CHURCH.

78.　　　　　*S. M.*　　　　*(Hymnal 191.)*

I LOVE Thy kingdom, Lord,
　　The house of Thine abode,
The Church our blest Redeemer saved
　　With His own precious blood.

2 I love Thy Church, O God ;
　　Her walls before Thee stand,
Dear as the apple of Thine eye,
　　And graven on Thy hand.

3 Beyond my highest joy
　　I prize her heavenly ways,
Her sweet communion, solemn vows,
　　Her hymns of love and praise.

4 Jesus, Thou Friend divine,
　　Our Saviour and our King,
Thy hand from every snare and foe
　　Shall great deliverance bring.

5 Sure as Thy truth shall last,
　　To Sion shall be given

The brightest glories earth can yield,
    And brighter bliss of Heaven.   Amen.

79.   *8s. 7s., double.*   *(Hymnal 190.)*

GLORIOUS things of thee are spoken,
    Zion, city of our God :
He, Whose word cannot be broken,
    Form'd thee for His own abode ;
On the Rock of Ages founded,
    What can shake thy sure repose ?
With salvation's walls surrounded,
    Thou may'st smile at all thy foes.

2 See, the streams of living waters,
    Springing from eternal love,
Well supply thy sons and daughters,
    And all fear of want remove !
Who can faint, while such a river
    Ever flows their thirst to assuage ?
Grace, which like the Lord, the giver,
    Never fails from age to age.

3 Round each habitation hovering,
    See the cloud and fire appear,
For a glory and a covering,
    Showing that the Lord is near.
Blest inhabitants of Zion,
    Wash'd in the Redeemer's blood !

Jesus, whom their souls rely on,
    Makes them kings and priests to God.
                                AMEN.

VII.—BAPTISM.

80.   *8s. 7s. 4.*

WHEN of old the Jewish mothers
        Brought their little babes to Thee,
To Thy stern Apostles' chiding,
    Thou didst answer tenderly;
        ‖: Gentle Jesus, :‖
    " Suffer them to come to Me."

2 To Thee given, from Thee naméd,
    Ransomed Christian children, we
Press around to share Thy blessing,
    Plead Thy mercy, full and free ;
        ‖: Gentle Jesus, :‖
    " Suffer us to come to Thee."

3 By Thy sign upon our forehead
    When Thy people bowed the knee ;
By the Name above us spoken,
    Of the wondrous Trinity ;
        ‖: Gentle Jesus, :‖
    " Suffer us to come to Thee."

4 By each prayer, and by each promise,
    When our hearts are full of glee ;

When our little sorrows vex us,
    Thine in all things we would be.
      ‖: Gentle Jesus, :‖
  "Suffer us to come to Thee."   Amen.

81.   *C. M.*   .   *(Hymnal 214.)*

IN token that thou shalt not fear
    Christ crucified to own,
We print the Cross upon thee here
    And stamp thee His alone.

2 In token that thou shalt not blush
    To glory in His Name,
We blazon here upon thy front
    His glory and His shame.

3 In token that thou shalt not flinch,
    Christ's quarrel to maintain,
But 'neath His banner manfully
    Firm at thy post remain ;

4 In token that thou too shalt tread
    The path He travelled by,
Endure the cross, despise the shame,
    And sit thee down on high ;

5 Thus outwardly and visibly
    We seal thee for His own ;
And may the brow that wears His cross
    Hereafter share His crown.   Amen

82. *L. M.* *(Hymnal 218.)*

JESUS, and shall it ever be,
 A mortal man ashamed of Thee !
Ashamed of Thee, whom angels praise,
Whose glories shine through endless days?

2 Ashamed of Jesus ! sooner far
Let night disown each radiant star ;
'T is midnight with my soul, till He,
Bright Morning Star, bid darkness flee.

3 Ashamed of Jesus ! O as soon
Let morning blush to own the sun ;
He sheds the beams of light divine
O'er this benighted soul of mine.

4 Ashamed of Jesus ! that dear Friend
On Whom my hopes of heaven depend ?
No ; when I blush, be this my shame,
That I no more revere His Name.

5 Ashamed of Jesus ! sinful pride ;
I'll boast a Saviour crucified :
And oh ! may this my portion be,
My Saviour not ashamed of me.   AMEN.

VIII.—INVITATION AND WARNING.

83.

REMEMBER thy Creator now,
   In these, thy youthful days ;
He will accept thine earliest vow ;
He loves thine earliest praise.
Chorus.—Remember thou, remember thou,
      He will accept thine earliest vow ;
      He loves thine earliest praise.

2 Remember thy Creator now,
   Seek Him while He is near ;
For evil days will come when thou
   Shalt find no comfort here.
Chorus.—Remember thou, remember thou,
      For evil days will come when thou
      Shalt find no comfort here.

3 Remember thy Creator now,
   His willing servant be ;
Then when thy head in death shall bow,
   He will remember thee.
Chorus.—Remember thou, remember thou,
      Then, when thy head in death shall bow
      He will remember thee.

4 Almighty God ! our hearts incline
   Thy heavenly voice to hear ;

Let all our future days be Thine,
    Devoted to Thy fear.
Chorus.—Remember us, remember us;
        Let all our future days be Thine
        Devoted to Thy fear.   Amen.

84.   *7s. 6s., double, with chorus.*

GO thou in life's fair morning,
    Go, in thy bloom of youth,
And seek for thine adorning,
    The precious pearl of truth :
Secure the heav'nly treasure,
    And bind it on thy heart ;
And let no earthly pleasure
    E'er cause it to depart.
Chorus.—Go thou in life's fair morning,
        Go, in thy bloom of youth,
        And seek for thine adorning
        The precious pearl of truth.

2 Go, while the day-star shineth,
    Go, while thy heart is light,
Go, ere thy strength declineth,
    While every sense is bright :
Sell all thou hast and buy it ;
    'T is worth all earthly things,—
Rubies, and gold, and diamonds,
    Sceptres and crowns of kings !—*Chor.*

3 Go, ere the cloud of sorrow
    Steals o'er thy bloom of youth;
Defer not till to-morrow;
    Go, now and buy the truth.
Go, seek thy great Creator;
    Learn early to be wise;
Go, place upon the altar,
    A morning sacrifice.—*Chor.*   AMEN.

85.

‖: OH, won't you be a Christian
        While you 're young? :‖
Don't think it will be better
To delay it until later,
But remember your Creator
        While you 're young.

2 ‖: Oh, won't you love the Saviour
        While you 're young? :‖
For you He left His glory
And embraced His cross so gory;
Won't you heed the melting story
        While you 're young?

3 ‖: Remember, death may find you
        While you 're young: :‖
For friends are often weeping,
And the stars their watch are keeping
O'er the grassy graves, where sleeping
        Lie the young.

4 ‖: Oh, walk the path of glory
     While you 're young! :‖
And Jesus will befriend you,
And from danger will defend you,
And a peace divine will send you
     While you 're young.   AMEN.

86.   *11s., with chorus.*

THE Master is coming, He calleth for thee,
  And loved ones are hast'ning their Saviour
    to see ;
He 's full of compassion, why will you delay ?
He 's calling, still calling, oh ! come, come
    away.

Chorus.—The Master is coming, He calleth for
     thee,
     Come, trust in His mercy, salvation is
     free.

2 The Master is coming ! receive Him and live :
Oh ! will you not trust Him your sins to forgive ?
On Calvary's mountain 'mid anguish and pain,
Thy ransom was purchased when Jesus was
    slain.—*Chor.*

3 The Master is coming, He calleth to-day !
Awake from thy slumbers to labor and pray ;

The morning is breaking, the noon-tide is near,
The evening's dark shadows will quickly ap-
    pear.—*Chor.*

4 The Master is coming, to call from the grave
His loved ones to glory; He's mighty to save;
And all who believe Him, in rapture shall sing
Salvation through Jesus, our Master and King.
  —*Chor.*   Amen.

87.   *S. M.*   *(Hymnal 134.)*

THE Spirit, in our hearts,
  Is whispering, Sinner, come:
The Bride, the Church of Christ, proclaims
  To all His children, Come.

2 Let him that heareth, say
  To all about him, Come:
Let him that thirsts for righteousness
  To Christ, the fountain, come.

3 Yes, whosoever will,
  - O let him freely come,
And freely drink the stream of life:
  'T is Jesus bids him come.

4 Lo, Jesus, who invites,
  Declares, I quickly come.
Lord! even so; I wait Thy hour;
  Jesus, my Saviour, come.   Amen.

88. *C. M.* *(Hymnal 222.)*

O HAPPY is the man who hears
  Religion's warning voice,
And who celestial wisdom makes
  His early, only choice.

2 For she has treasures greater far
  Than east or west unfold ;
More precious are her bright rewards,
  Than gems, or stores of gold.

3 Her right hand offers to the just
  Immortal, happy days ;
Her left, imperishable wealth,
  And heavenly crowns displays.

4 And, as her holy labors rise,
  So her rewards increase ;
Her ways are ways of pleasantness,
  And all her paths are peace. AMEN.

IX.—THE CHRISTIAN LIFE.

REPENTANCE.

89.

MY Saviour stands waiting, and knocks at
  the door ;
Has knocked and is knocking again ;

I hear His kind voice, I 'll reject Him no **more,**
Nor let Him stand pleading in vain.
In infinite mercy He came from above
To ransom, to cleanse me from sin,
I 'll yield to the voice of His merciful love,
And let my dear Saviour come in.

Chorus.—Saviour, come in ! cleanse me from sin !
Jesus, my Saviour, come in, come in !
Enter the door,
Waiting no more,
Saviour, dear Saviour, come in !

2 O Saviour, my Ransom, Redeemer and Friend,
The Life, and the Truth, and the Way,
On Thy precious merit alone I depend ;
Dwell in me and keep me, I pray.
Thy goodness hath opened the door **of my**
heart—
'T is open in welcome to Thee ;
Come in, Blessed Saviour, and never depart ;
Come in, with Thy mercy, to me.—*Chor.*

AMEN.

90.   8s. 6.   *(Hymnal 392.)*

JUST as I am—without one plea,
But that Thy blood was shed for me,
And that Thou bidd'st me come to Thee,
O Lamb of God, I come.

2 Just as I am—and waiting not
  To rid my soul of one dark blot ;
  To Thee, Whose blood can cleanse each spot,
      O Lamb of God, I come.

3 Just as I am—though tossed about
  With many a conflict, many a doubt,
  With fears within, and foes without,
      O Lamb of God, I come.

4 Just as I am—poor, wretched, blind—
  Sight, riches, healing of the mind,
  Yea, all I need, in Thee to find,
      O Lamb of God, I come.

5 Just as I am—Thou wilt receive,
  Wilt welcome, pardon, cleanse, relieve ;
  Because Thy promise I believe,
      O Lamb of God, I come.

6 Just as I am—Thy love unknown
  Has broken every barrier down ;
  Now to be Thine, yea, Thine alone,
      O Lamb of God, I come.   AMEN.

91.   *7s. 6s., double.*   *(Hymnal 10.)*

O JESU, Thou art standing
    Outside the fast-closed door,
  In lowly patience waiting
    To pass the threshold o'er :

We bear the name of Christians,
  His Name and sign we bear:
O shame, thrice shame upon us,
  To keep Him standing there.

2 O Jesu, Thou art knocking:
  And lo! that hand is scarr'd,
And thorns Thy brow encircle,
  And tears Thy face have marr'd
O love that passeth knowledge,
  So patiently to wait!
O sin that hath no equal,
  So fast to bar the gate!

3 O Jesu, Thou art pleading
  In accents meek and low,
"I died for you, My children,
  And will ye treat Me so?"
O Lord, with shame and sorrow
  We open now the door:
Dear Saviour, enter, enter,
  And leave us nevermore.   AMEN

92.   *7s. 6s., double.*

WHAT shall I do with Jesus,
  The Christ Who may be mine?
Accept Him as my Saviour,
  Or spurn the gift divine?

His only Son God gave me—
I must, I do decide ;
And Christ I take to save me,
Or Christ is now denied.

2 What shall I do with Jesus,
The precious Lamb of God ?
I cast my soul upon Him—
He bathes it in His blood ;
I 'll gratefully confess Him
Before the vile and just ;
My ransomed powers shall bless Him,
My sure and only trust.

3 What shall I do with Jesus ?
For Him the cross I 'll take ;
All earthly losses suffer,
Ere I the Lord forsake.
In scenes of joy and sighing,
His love shall be the same ;
While living and in dying
I 'll glory in His Name.   AMEN.

FAITH.

93.   *7s., double.*   *(Hymnal 393.)*

JESU, Lover of my soul,
Let me to Thy bosom fly,

While the nearer waters roll,
   While the tempest still is high:
Hide me, O my Saviour, hide,
   Till the storm of life be past;
Safe into the haven guide;
   O receive my soul at last.

2 Other refuge have I none,
   Hangs my helpless soul on Thee:
Leave, ah! leave me not alone,
   Still support and comfort me:
All my trust on Thee is stay'd,
   All my hope from Thee I bring;
Cover my defenceless head
   With the shadow of Thy wing.

3 Plenteous grace with Thee is found,
   Grace to cover all my sin;
Let the healing streams abound,
   Make and keep me pure within:
Thou of life the fountain art,
   Freely let me take of Thee:
Spring Thou up within my heart,
   Rise to all eternity.   AMEN.

94.   *Six 7s.*   *(Hymnal* 391.*)*

ROCK of Ages, cleft for me,
   Let me hide myself in Thee;

Let the water and the blood,
From Thy riven side which flow'd,
Be of sin the double cure,
Cleanse me from its guilt and power.

2 Not the labors of my hands
Can fulfill Thy law's demands ;
Could my zeal no respite know,
Could my tears for ever flow,
All for sin could not atone,
Thou must save, and Thou alone.

3 Nothing in my hand I bring ;
Simply to Thy cross I cling ;
Naked, come to Thee for dress ;
Helpless, look to Thee for grace :
Foul, I to the Fountain fly ;
Wash me, Saviour, or I die.

4 While I draw this fleeting breath,
When my eyelids close in death,
When I soar through tracts unknown,
See Thee on Thy judgment throne,—
Rock of Ages, cleft for me,
Let me hide myself in Thee.   Amen.

HOPE.

95.   *C. M.*   *(Hymnal 476.)*

AWAKE, my soul, stretch every nerve,
  And press with vigor on ;

A heavenly race demands thy zeal,
  And an immortal crown.

2 A cloud of witnesses around
  Hold thee in full survey;
Forget the steps already trod,
  And onward urge thy way.

3 'T is God's all-animating voice
  That calls thee from on high,
'T is His own hand presents the prize
  To thine aspiring eye.

4 Then wake, my soul, stretch every nerve,
  And press with vigor on;
A heavenly race demands thy zeal,
  And an immortal crown.   AMEN.

96.   *7s. 6s., double.*   (*Hymnal* 447.)

RISE, my soul, and stretch thy wings,
  Thy better portion trace;
Rise, from transitory things,
  Towards heaven, thy native place:
Sun, and moon, and stars decay,
  Time shall soon this earth remove;
Rise, my soul, and haste away
  To seats prepared above.

2 Cease, my soul, O cease to mourn,
  Press onward to the prize;

Soon thy Saviour will return,.
  To take thee to the skies :
There, is everlasting peace,
  Rest, enduring rest, in heaven ;
There will sorrow ever cease,
  And crowns of joy be given.   AMEN.

PRAYER.

97.　　　　　　　*C. M.*　　　　*(Hymnal 404.)*

PRAYER is the soul's sincere desire,
  Utter'd or unexpress'd ;
The motion of a hidden fire,
  That trembles in the breast.

2 Prayer is the burden of a sigh,
    The falling of a tear ;
The upward glancing of an eye,
    When none but God is near.

3 Prayer is the simplest form of speech
    That infant lips can try ;
Prayer, the sublimest strains that reach
    The Majesty on high.

4 Prayer is the contrite sinner's voice,
    Returning from his ways ;
While angels in their songs rejoice,
    And cry, " Behold, he prays !"

5 O Thou, by Whom we come to God,
The Life, the Truth, the Way,
The path of prayer Thyself hast trod;
Lord, teach us how to pray.   AMEN.

98.   *7s. 6s., double, with chorus.*

GO when the morning shineth,
Go when the noon is bright,
Go when the eve declineth,
Go in the hush of night:
Go with pure mind and feeling,
Fling earthly thought away,
And in thy closet, kneeling,
Do thou in secret pray.

Chorus.—Go when the morning shineth,
Go when the noon is bright,
Go when the eve declineth,
Go in the hush of night.

2 Remember all who love thee,
All who are loved by thee;
Pray, too, for those who hate thee,
If any such there be:
Then for thyself, in meekness,
A blessing humbly claim,
And blend with each petition
Thy great Redeemer's name.—*Chor.*

3 Or, if 't is e'er denied thee
    In solitude to pray,
  Should holy thoughts come o'er thee
    When friends are round thy way,
  E'en then the silent breathing,
    Thy spirit raised above,
  Will reach His throne of glory,
    Where dwells eternal love.—*Chor.*

4 Oh! not a joy or blessing
    With this can we compare—
  The grace our Father gives us,
    To pour our souls in prayer :
  Whene'er thou art in sadness,
    Before His footstool fall ;
  Remember, in thy gladness,
    His love who gave thee all.—*Chor.* Amen.

99.

OUR | Father Who | art in | heaven, |
  Hallow-ed | be Thy | Name ; |
Thy kingdom | come, |
Thy will be | done on | earth
As it | is in | heaven : |
Give us this | day our | daily | bread,
And for- | give us our | trespasses
As | we forgive | them that | trespass a- |
    gainst | us : ‖
Duett. And | lead us | not into temp | tation

But de- | liver us from | evil : ‖
Chorus. For | Thine is the | kingdom
And the | power and the | glory
For | ever and | ever and | ever A· |
    men ;
For | ever and | ever and | ever | A- | men.

PRAISE.

100.   *C. M.*   *(Hymnal 424.)*

ALL hail the power of Jesu's Name !
  Let angels prostrate fall ;
Bring forth the royal diadem
    And crown Him !
      Crown Him !
      Crown Him !
    Crown Him Lord of all !

2 Crown Him, ye martyrs of our God,
  Who from His altar call ;
Extol the stem of Jesse's rod,
    And crown Him ! Crown Him ! etc.

3 Hail Him, the heir of David's line,
  Whom David, Lord did call ;
The God Incarnate ! Man Divine !
    And crown Him ! Crown Him ! etc.

4 Ye seed of Israel's chosen race,
  Ye ransomed of the fall,

Hail Him Who saves you by His grace,
    And crown Him! Crown Him! etc.

5 Let every kindred, every tribe,
    On this terrestrial ball,
To Him all majesty ascribe,
    And crown Him! Crown Him! etc.
                  AMEN.

101.   *C. M., with chorus.*   *(Hymnal 395.)*

HOW sweet the Name of Jesus sounds
    In a believer's ear!
It soothes his sorrows, heals his wounds,
    And drives away his fear.

Chorus.—O who's like Jesus, Hallelujah!
        Praise ye the Lord :
           There's none like Jesus, Hallelujah!
        Love and serve the Lord.

2 It makes the wounded spirit whole,
    And calms the troubled breast ;
'T is manna to the hungry soul,
    And to the weary rest.—*Chor.*

3 Dear Name, the Rock on which I build,
    My Shield and Hiding-place,
My never-failing Treasury, filled
    With boundless stores of grace.—*Chor.*

4 Jesus ! my Shepherd, Husband, Friend,
      My Prophet, Priest, and King,
    My Lord, my Life, my Way, my End—
      Accept the praise I bring.—*Chor.*

5 Weak is the effort of my heart,
      And cold my warmest thought :
    But when I see Thee as Thou art,
      I 'll praise Thee as I ought.—*Chor.* AMEN.

102.

THE valleys and the mountains,
    The woodland and the plain,
The rivers and the fountains,
    The sunshine and the rain,
The stars that shine above me,
    The flowers that deck the sod,
Proclaim aloud the glory of my God.
    Praises, holy adoration,
Praises to the God above ;
    Praises thro' the wide creation,
Sound aloud His greatness and His love.

2 And shall the voice of nature
      Thus glorify its King ;
    And man, the noble creature,
      No grateful tribute bring ?
    Shall mercy strew his pathway,

And all the senses please,
And man withhold the sacrifice of praise?
  Praise Him, ye that live forever;
Praise Him, every heart and voice;
  Praise Him, He's the glorious Giver;
Praise Him in your sorrows and your joys.

3 The word of life He gave us
    To guide us to the sky;
  That He might justly save us,
    He sent His Son to die—
  To die in shame and anguish,
    To die a sacrifice;
  To save us from the death that never dies.
    Praise Him, praise Him for salvation;
  Praise Him, praise Him for His Son;
    Praise Him, every tribe and nation;
  Praise Him for the battle He has won.

4 Then train your youthful voices
    To hymn His praise above;
  For He who here rejoices
    In Jesus' dying love,
  Around His throne in glory
    Shall all His love proclaim,
  And sing the song of Moses and the Lamb.
    Praise Him, praise th' Eternal Father;
  Praise Him, praise th' Eternal Son;

Praise Him, praise the Three together,
Father, Son, and Spirit, Three in One.

AMEN.

103.   *7s., with chorus.*   *(Hymnal 422.)*

SONGS of praise the angels sang;
Heaven with Hallelujahs rang,
When Jehovah's work begun,
When He spake and it was done.

 Chorus.—Hallelujah! Hallelujah!
   Hallelujah!   Amen.

2 Songs of praise awoke the morn,
When the Prince of Peace was born;
Songs of praise arose, when He
Captive led captivity.—*Chor.*

3 Heaven and earth must pass away;
Songs of praise shall crown that day:
God will make new heavens and earth;
Songs of praise shall hail their birth.—*Chor.*

4 And shall man alone be dumb,
Till that glorious kingdom come?
No; the church delights to raise,
Psalms, and hymns, and songs of praise.—

Chor.

5 Saints below, with heart and voice,
Still in songs of praise rejoice;

108

Learning here by faith and love,
Songs of praise to sing above.—*Chor.*

6 Borne upon their latest breath,
Songs of praise shall conquer death ;
Then amidst eternal joy
Songs of praise their powers employ.—*Chor.*

104.   *6s. 5s., double.*

SAVIOUR, Blessèd Saviour,
     Listen whilst we sing ;
Hearts and voices raising
     Praises to our King.
All we have to offer ;
     All we hope to be ;
Body, soul, and spirit,
     All, we yield to Thee.

2 Nearer, ever nearer,
     Christ, we draw to Thee ;
Deep in adoration
     Bending low the knee :
Thou for our redemption
     Cam'st on earth to die ;
Thou, that we might follow,
     Hast gone up on high.

3 Great and ever greater
     Are Thy mercies here ·

True and everlasting
  Are the glories there,
Where no pain, or sorrow,
  Toil, or care is known,
Where the angel-legions
  Circle round Thy throne.

4 Brighter still and brighter
    Glows the western sun,
  Shedding all its gladness
    O'er our work that's done;
  Time will soon be over,
    Toil and sorrows past;
  May we, Blessèd Saviour,
    Find a rest at last.

5 Onward, ever onward,
    Journeying o'er the road
  Worn by saints before us,
    Journeying on to God:
  Leaving all behind us,
    May we hasten on,
  Backward never looking
    Till the prize is won.

6 Bliss, all bliss excelling,
    When the ransomed soul,
  Earthly toils forgetting,
    Finds its promised goal;

Where in joys unheard of
Saints with angels sing,
Never weary, raising
Praises to their King.   AMEN.

105.

Chorus.

WE praise Thee, we bless Thee !
Thou Who only art Divine ;
No name is worthy such homage as Thine ;
Our heart's adoration
Forever we will gladly bring
To Thee, our Redeemer, Creator, and King. ·

Semi-chorus.

To meet the glad echoes our voices we raise,
And join with our souls in the anthem of praise.

Chorus.

We praise Thee, we bless Thee !
Thou Who only art Divine;
For no name is worthy such homage as Thine.

Solo.

With angels in glory,
We herald the story,
Glad tidings of joy and peace
Thro' our Saviour and King.

Chorus.

We praise Thee, we bless Thee !
Thou Who only art Divine ;

No name is worthy such homage as Thine;
    Our heart's adoration
    Forever we will gladly bring
To Thee, our Redeemer, Creator, and King.

    Semi-chorus.

For mercies unnumbered, for tenderest care,
For blessings Thy children so bounteously share;
    Chorus.
    We praise Thee, we bless Thee!
    Thou Who only art Divine;
For no name is worthy such homage as Thine.
    Solo.
    Now joyfully blending,
    With rapture ascending,
    Our tribute of praise to Thee,
    Blessèd Saviour and King.
    Chorus.
    We praise Thee, we bless Thee!
    Thou, Who only art Divine;
No name is worthy such homage as Thine;
    Our heart's adoration
    Forever we will gladly bring
To Thee, our Redeemer, Creator, and King.

    Semi-chorus.

For all the sweet promises faithfully given,
For all the bright hopes that look forward to
    heaven:

Chorus.

We praise Thee, we bless Thee !
Thou, Who only art Divine ;
For no name is worthy such homage as **Thine.**

Solo.

Our hearts warmly glowing,
With melody flowing,
All glory and praise to Thee,
Blessèd Saviour and King.

Chorus.

We praise Thee, we bless Thee !
Thou, Who only art Divine ;
No name is worthy such homage as Thine ;
Our heart's adoration
Forever we will gladly bring
To Thee, our Redeemer, Creator, and **King.**

Semi-chorus.

Our voices in chorus exultingly rise,
To join with the angels whose songs fill the **skies**

Chorus.

We praise Thee, we bless Thee !
Thou, Who only art Divine ;
For no name is worthy such homage as **Thine.**

Solo.

Ye angels in glory,
Still herald the story,

Sing praises forevermore
To our Saviour and King.

Chorus.

We praise Thee, we bless Thee !
Thou, Who only art Divine ;
No name is worthy such homage as Thine.
Our heart's adoration
Forever we will gladly bring
To Thee, our Creator, Redeemer, and King.
Hallelujah ! Hallelujah ! Hallelujah ! Amen.
Hallelujah ! Hallelujah ! Hallelujah ! Amen.
Hallelujah ! Amen. Amen.

106.　　　　8s. 7s.　　　　*(Hymnal 423.)*

GOD, my King, Thy might confessing,
　　Ever will I bless Thy Name ;
Day by day Thy throne addressing,
　　Still will I Thy praise proclaim.

2 Honor great our God befitteth ;
　　Who His majesty can reach ?
Age to age His works transmitteth,
　　Age to age His power shall teach.

3 They shall talk of all Thy glory,
　　On Thy might and greatness dwell ;
Speak of Thy dread acts the story
　　And Thy deeds of wonder tell.

4 Nor shall fail from memory's treasure,
    Works by love and mercy wrought;
  Works of love surpassing measure,
    Works of mercy passing thought.   AMEN.

107.   8s. 7s., *double.*   (*Hymnal* 454.)

LORD, with glowing heart I'd praise Thee
    For the bliss Thy love bestows,
For the pardoning grace that saves me,
    And the peace that from it flows:
Help, O God, my weak endeavor;
    This dull soul to rapture raise:
Thou must light the flame, or never
    Can my love be warmed to praise.

2 Praise, my soul, the God that sought thee,
    Wretched wanderer, far astray;
  Found thee lost, and kindly brought thee
    From the paths of death away;
  Praise with love's devoutest feeling,
    Him Who saw thy guilt-born fear,
  And, the light of hope revealing,
    Bade the blood-stained cross appear.

3 Lord, this bosom's ardent feeling
    Vainly would my lips express:
  Low before Thy footstool kneeling,
    Deign Thy suppliant's prayer to bless:

Let Thy grace, my soul's chief treasure,
  Love's pure flame within me raise,
And, since words can never measure,
  Let my life show forth Thy praise.   AMEN.

108.   8s. 7s.   *(Hymnal 370.)*

SAVIOUR, source of every blessing,
  Tune my heart to grateful lays;
Streams of mercy, never ceasing,
  Call for ceaseless songs of praise.

    Chorus.—Hallelujah! Hallelujah!
        Hallelujah! Amen.

2 Teach me some melodious measure,
  Sung by raptured saints above;
Fill my soul with sacred pleasure,
  While I sing redeeming love.—*Chor.*

3 Thou didst seek me when a stranger,
  Wandering from the fold of God;
Thou, to save my soul from danger,
  Didst redeem me with Thy blood.—*Chor.*

4 By Thy hand restored, defended,
  Safe through life thus far I've come;
Safe, O Lord, when life is ended,
  Bring me to my heavenly home.—*Chor.*
                    AMEN.

109. *S. M.* *(Hymnal 413.)*

O BLESS the Lord, my soul,
  His grace to thee proclaim ;
And all that is within me, join
  To bless His holy Name.

2 O bless the Lord, my soul,
  His mercies bear in mind ;
Forget not all His benefits,
  Who is to thee so kind.

3 He pardons all thy sins,
  Prolongs thy feeble breath ,
He healeth thine infirmities,
  And ransoms thee from death.

4 He feeds thee with His love,
  Upholds thee with His truth ;
And, like the eagle's, He renews
  The vigor of thy youth.

5 Then bless the Lord, my soul,
  His grace, His love proclaim ;
Let all that is within me, join
  To bless His holy Name. AMEN.

DOING GOOD.

110.

WORK, for the night is coming,
  Work thro' the morning hours,

Work, while the dew is sparkling,
Work 'mid springing flow'rs.

2 Work, for the night is coming,
Work thro' the sunny noon;
Fill brightest hours with labor,
Rest comes sure and soon.

3 Work for the night is coming,
Under the sunset skies;
While their bright tints are glowing,
Work, for daylight flies.   AMEN.

111.   *8s. 7s., double.*

IF you cannot on the .ocean
Sail among the swiftest fleet,
Rocking on the highest billows,
Laughing at the storms you meet,
You can stand among the sailors,
Anchor'd yet within the bay;
You can lend a hand to help them
As they launch their boat away.

2 If you are too weak to journey
Up the mountain, steep and high,
You can stand within the valley,
While the multitudes go by;
You can chaunt in happy measures,
As they slowly pass along;

Though they may forget the singer,
  They will not forget the song.

3 If you have not gold or silver
    Ever ready to command ;
  If you cannot t'ward the needy
    Reach an ever open hand ;
  You can visit the afflicted,
    O'er the erring you can weep ;
  You can be a true disciple
    Sitting at the Saviour's feet.

4 If you cannot in the harvest
    Garner up the richest sheaves,
  Many a grain both ripe and golden
    Will the careless reapers leave ;
  Go and glean among the briers,
    Growing rank against the wall,
  For it may be that their shadow
    Hides the heaviest wheat of all.

5 If you cannot in the conflict
    Prove yourself a soldier true—
  If where fire and smoke are thickest,
    There 's no work for you to do ;
  When the battle-field is silent,
    You can go with careful tread,
  You can bear away the wounded,
    You can cover up the dead.

6 Do not, then, stand idly waiting,
　For some greater work to do ;
Fortune is a lazy goddess—
　She will never come to you.
Go and toil in any vineyard,
　Do not fear to do or dare ;
If you want a field of labor,
　You can find it anywhere.　　　AMEN.

112.　　　　　8s. 7s. 4.　　　*(Hymnal 227.)*

IN the vineyard of our Father
　Daily work we find to do ;
Scatter'd gleanings we may gather,
　Though we are but young and few ;
　　‖: Little clusters :‖
Help to fill the garners too.

2 Toiling early in the morning,
　Catching moments through the day,
Nothing small or lowly scorning,
　While we work, and watch, and pray ;
　　‖: Gathering gladly :‖
Free-will offerings by the way.

3 Not for selfish praise or glory,
　Not for objects nothing worth,
But to send the blessèd story
　Of the Gospel o'er the earth ;

‖: Telling mortals :‖
Of our Lord and Saviour's birth.

4 Steadfast, then, in our endeavor,
    Heavenly Father, may we be ;
And for ever, and for ever,
    We will give the praise to Thee ;
    ‖: Hallelujah :‖
Singing, all eternity.   AMEN.

RESISTING EVIL.

113.   *6s. 5s., double, with chorus.*

FIGHT the good fight bravely,
    Yield not to the foe !
In the van of battle
    Strike the Victor's blow !
Jesus watcheth o'er you,
    Do not be afraid !
Gird on all your armor,
    Never be dismayed.

Chorus.—Fight the good fight bravely !
        Conquer far and wide !
        Fight the good fight nobly,
        ‖: God is on your side ! :‖

2 Fight the good fight nobly,
    Heed the tempter not !

In the march to vict'ry
Be our toils forgot !
Onward still, and upward !
Fear not slight nor frown !
Soon in joy and triumph,
Ye shall wear the crown !—*Chor.*

AMEN.

114.   *C. M.*   *(Hymnal 471.)*

AM I a soldier of the cross,
A follower of the Lamb ?
And shall I fear to own His cause,
Or blush to speak His Name ?

2 Must I be carried to the skies
On flowery beds of ease,
While others fought to win the prize,
And sailed through bloody seas ?

3 Are there no foes for me to face ?
Must I not stem the flood ?
Is the gay world a friend to grace,
To help me on to God ?

4 Sure I must fight if I would reign ;
Increase my courage, Lord ;
I 'll bear the cross, endure the pain,
Supported by Thy word.   AMEN.

115.　　　　*S. M.*　　　*(Hymnal 216.)*

SOLDIERS of Christ, arise,
　And put your armor on,
Strong in the strength which God supplies
　Through His eternal Son.

2 Strong in the Lord of hosts,
　And in His mighty power;
Who in the strength of Jesus trusts,
　Is more than conqueror.

3 Stand then in His great might,
　With all His strength endued;
And take, to arm you for the fight,
　The panoply of God.

4 That having all things done,
　And all your conflicts past,
Ye may behold your victory won,
　And stand complete at last.　　　AMEN.

116.

SOUND the battle-cry!
　See, the foe is nigh!
Raise the standard high
　For the Lord:
Gird your armor on,
　Stand firm, every one;
Rest your cause upon
　His holy word.

Chorus.
Rouse, then, soldiers ! Rally round the banner !
Ready ! steady ! Pass the word along.
Onward ! forward ! Shout aloud, Hosannah !
Christ is Captain of the mighty throng.

2 Strong to meet the foe,
  Marching on we go,
While our cause, we know,
  Must prevail.
Shield and banner bright
  Gleaming in the light,
Battling for the right
  We ne'er can fail.—*Chor.*

3 O Thou God of all,
  Hear us when we call ;
Help us, one and all,
  By Thy grace ;
When the battle's done,
  And the victory won,
May we wear the crown
  Before Thy face.—*Chor.*   AMEN.

CHRISTIAN LIFE IN GENERAL.

117.   *(Hymnal 507.)*

NEARER, my God, to Thee,
    Nearer to Thee,

E'en though it be a cross
That raiseth me ;
Still all my song shall be,
Nearer, my God, to Thee,
Nearer to Thee.

2 Though like the wanderer,
The sun gone down,
Darkness comes over me,
My rest a stone ;
Yet in my dreams I 'd be
Nearer, my God, to Thee,
Nearer to Thee.

3 There let my way appear
Steps unto heaven ;
All that Thou sendest me
In mercy given ;
Angels to beckon me
Nearer, my God, to Thee,
Nearer to Thee.

4 Then with my waking thoughts,
Bright with Thy praise,
Out of my stony griefs
Altars I 'll raise ;
So by my woes to be
Nearer, my God, to Thee,
Nearer to Thee.

5 Or if on joyful wing.
    Cleaving the sky,
  Sun, moon, and stars forgot,
    Upward I fly ;
  Still all my song shall be,
  Nearer, my God, to Thee,
    Nearer to Thee.   AMEN.

118.   *L. M.*

O LORD, young martyrs, brave and true,
    Have yielded up for Thee their life,
  And children's bodies, weak as ours,
    Have dared for Thee the fire and strife.

2 We wear the cross they wore of old,
    Our lips have learned like vows to make ;
  We need not die ; we may not fight ;
    What can we do for Jesus' sake ?

3 O day by day each Christian child
    Has much to do, without, within ;
  A death to die for Jesus' sake,
    A ceaseless war to wage with sin.

4 When deep within our swelling hearts,
    The thoughts of pride and anger rise,
  When bitter words are on our tongues,
    And tears of passion in our eyes ;

5 Then we may stay the angry blow,
  Then we may check the hasty word,
Give gentle answers back again,
  And fight a battle for our Lord.

6 With smiles of peace and looks of love,
  Light in our dwellings we may make ;
Bid kind good-humor brighten there,
  And do all still for Jesus' sake.

7 There's not a child so small and weak
  But has his little cross to take,
His little work of love and praise
  That he may do for Jesus' sake.   AMEN.

119.

MY Father, I would be Thy child,
  I know I 'm sinful, wayward, wild ;
To Thee I would be reconciled ;
Oh ! make me, oh ! make me Thine.

2 With patience I the race would run,
  Not looking back when once begun,
And seek salvation through Thy Son ;
Oh ! make me, oh ! make me Thine.

3 The narrow way I fain would tread,
  And by Thy gentle hand be led,
With heavenly manna daily fed ;
Oh ! make me, oh ! make me Thine.

4 Make me to love Thee more and more,
  Thy Holy Spirit on me pour ;
  Thy holy Name may I adore ;
  Oh! make me, oh! make me Thine. Amen

120.   8s. 7s. 4.

GOD has said, " Forever blessèd
    Those who seek me in their youth—
They shall find the path of wisdom,
    And the narrow way of truth :"
      ‖: Guide us, Saviour, :‖
In the narrow way of truth.

2 Be our strength, for we are weakness ;
    Be our wisdom and our guide ;
May we walk in love and meekness,
    Nearer to our Saviour's side ;
      ‖: Nought can harm us, :‖
While we thus in Thee abide.

3 Thus, when evening shades shall gather,
    We may turn our tearless eye
  To the dwelling of our Father,
    To our home beyond the sky ;—
      ‖: Gently passing, :‖
  · To that brighter world on high.   Amen

121.　　　　8s. 7s. 4.　　　*(Hymnal 506.)*

LEAD us, Heavenly Father, lead us
　　O'er the world's tempestuous sea ;
Guard us, guide us, keep us, feed us,
　For we have no help but Thee :
　　　Yet possessing
　　　Every blessing,
If our God our Father be.

2 Saviour, breathe forgiveness o'er us ;
　All our weakness Thou dost know ;
Thou didst tread this earth before us,
　Thou didst feel its keenest woe ;
　　　Lone and dreary,
　　　Faint and weary,
Through the desert Thou didst go.

3 Spirit of our God, descending,
　Fill our hearts with heavenly joy ;
Love with every passion blending,
　Pleasure that can never cloy :
　　　Thus provided
　　　Pardon'd, guided,
Nothing can our peace destroy.　　Amen.

122.　　　　*C. M.*　　　*(Hymnal 501.)*

THOU art the Way, to Thee alone
　From sin and death we flee ;

And he who would the Father seek,
Must seek Him, Lord, by Thee.

2 Thou art the Truth, Thy word alone
True wisdom can impart;
Thou only canst inform the mind
And purify the heart.

3 Thou art the Life, the rending tomb
Proclaims Thy conquering arm;
And those who put their trust in Thee
Nor death nor hell shall harm.

4 Thou art the Way, the Truth, the Life;
Grant us that way to know,
That truth to keep, that life to win,
Where joys eternal flow.   AMEN.

123.   *(Hymnal 472.)*

BREAST the wave, Christian,
When it is strongest;
Watch for day, Christian,
When the night's longest;
Onward and onward still,
Be thine endeavor;
The rest that remaineth
Will be for ever.

2 Fight the fight, Christian,
Jesus is o'er Thee;

Run the race, Christian,
　　Heaven is before thee ;
He Who hath promisèd,
　　Faltereth never ;
He Who hath loved so well,
　　Loveth for ever.

3 Lift thine eye, Christian,
　　Just as it closeth ;
Raise thy heart, Christian,
　　Ere it reposeth ;
Thee from the love of Christ,
　　Nothing shall sever ;
And when Thy work is done,
　　Praise Him for ever.　　　　AMEN.

124.　　　　　*D. S. M.*　　　*(Hymnal 434.)*

JESUS, my strength, my hope,
　　On Thee I cast my care,
With humble confidence, look up,
　　And know Thou hear'st my prayer :
Give me on Thee to wait,
Till I can all things do—
On Thee, Almighty, to create,
　　Almighty to renew.

2　　　Give me a sober mind,
　　A self-renouncing will,

That tramples down and casts behind
The baits of pleasing ill :
A soul inured to pain,
To hardships, grief, and loss ;
Ready to take up and sustain
The consecrated cross.

3   Give me a godly fear
A quick, discerning eye,
That looks to Thee when sin is near,
And sees the tempter fly :
A spirit still prepared,
And armed with jealous care,
For ever standing on its guard,
And watching unto prayer.

4   I rest upon Thy word,
The promise is for me ;
My succor and salvation, Lord,
Shall surely come from Thee :
But let me still abide,
Nor from my hope remove,
Till Thou my patient spirit guide
Into Thy perfect love.   AMEN.

125.   *Six 7s.*

WORDS are things of little cost,
Quickly spoken, quickly lost ;

We forget them, but they stand
Witnesses at God's right hand :
And their testimony bear
For us, or against us there.

2 O, how often ours have been
Idle words and words of sin !
Words of anger, scorn, or pride,
Or deceit, our faults to hide ;
Envious tales, or strife unkind,
Leaving bitter thoughts behind.

3 Grant us, Lord, from day to day,
Strength to watch, and grace to pray :
May our lips, from sin kept free,
Love to speak and sing of Thee ;
Till in Heaven we learn to raise
Songs of everlasting praise.   Amen.

126.   *D. S. M.*

I WAS a wandering sheep,
    I did not love the fold ;
I did not love my Shepherd's voice,
    I would not be controlled.
I was a wayward child,
    I did not love my home ;
I did not love my Father's voice,
    I loved afar to roam.

2 The shepherd sought his sheep,
    The Father sought His child,
And follow'd me o'er vale and hill,
    O'er desert waste and wild.
He found me nigh to death,
    Famish'd and faint and lone ;
He bound me with the bands of love,
    And saved the wand'ring one.

3 He spoke in tender love,
    He raised my drooping head ;
He gently closed my bleeding wounds,
    My fainting soul He fed.
He wash'd my stains away,
    He made me clean and fair,
He brought me to my home in peace,
    The long-sought wanderer.

4 Jesus my Shepherd is,
    'T was He that loved my soul,
'T was He that wash'd me in His blood,
    'T was He that made me whole.
'T was He that sought the lost,
    That found the wandering sheep,
'T was He that brought me to the fold,
    'T is He that still doth keep.

5 I was a wandering sheep,
    I would not be controlled ;

But now I love my Shepherd's voice,
 I love, I love the fold!
I was a wayward child;
 I once preferred to roam,
But now I love my Father's voice;
 I love, I love His home! AMEN.

127. 8s. 7s. 4. *(Hymnal 229.)*

SAVIOUR, like a shepherd lead us,
 Much we need Thy tender care;
In Thy pleasant pastures feed us;
 For our use Thy folds prepare:
  ‖: Blessèd Jesus!
  Blessèd Jesus!
Thou hast bought us, Thine we are. :‖

2 Thou hast promised to receive us,
 Poor and sinful though we be;
Thou hast mercy to relieve us;
 Grace to cleanse, and power to free.
  ‖: Blessèd Jesus!
  Blessèd Jesus!
Let us early turn to Thee. :‖

3 Early let us seek Thy favor,
 Early let us learn Thy will;
Do Thou, Lord, our only Saviour,
 With Thy love our bosoms fill:

‖: Blessèd Jesus !
Blessèd Jesus !
Thou hast loved us,—love us still. :‖

AMEN.

128.   *8s. 7s., double.*

SITTING at the feet of Jesus,
  Oh, what words I hear Him say!
Happy place! so near, so precious!
  May it find me there each day!
Sitting at the feet of Jesus,
  I would look upon the past;
For His love has been so gracious,
  It has won my heart at last.

2 Sitting at the feet of Jesus,
  Where can mortal be more blest?
There I lay my sins and sorrows,
  And when weary, find sweet rest.
Sitting at the feet of Jesus,—
  There I love to sing and pray;
While I from His fullness gather
  Grace and comfort every day.

3 Bless me, O my Saviour! bless me,
  As I sit low at Thy feet;
O look down in love upon me;
  Let me see Thy face so sweet!

Give me, Lord, the mind of Jesus ;
  Make me holy as He is ;
May I prove I 've been with Jesus,
  Who is all my righteousness !   AMEN

129.   *7s. 6s., double.*

I LAY my sins on Jesus,
  The spotless Lamb of God ;
He bears them all, and frees us
  From the accursèd load :
I bring my guilt to Jesus,
  To wash my crimson stains
|: White in His blood most precious,
  Till not a spot remains. :|

2 I lay my wants on Jesus,
  All fullness dwells in Him ;
He healeth my diseases,
  He doth my soul redeem :
I lay my griefs on Jesus,
  My burdens and my cares ;
|: He from them all releases,
  He all my sorrow shares. :|

3 I long to be like Jesus,
  Meek, loving, lowly, mild ;
I long to be like Jesus,
  The Father's holy Child :

I hope to be with Jesus,
    Amid the Heavenly throng,
‖: To sing with saints His praises,
    And learn the angels' song. :‖   AMEN

130.   *(Hymnal 514.)*

ART thou weary, art thou languid,
    Art thou sore distress'd ?
"Come to me," saith One, *" and coming,
    Be at rest !"*

2 Hath He marks to lead me to Him,
    If He be my guide?
*"In His Feet and Hands are wound-prints,
    And His side."*

3 Is there diadem, as Monarch
    That His brow adorns?
*" Yea, a crown, in very surety,—
    But of thorns."*

4 If I find Him, if I follow,
    What His guerdon here?
*"Many a sorrow, many a labor,
    Many a tear."*

5 If I still hold closely to Him,
    What hath He at last?
*" Sorrow vanquished, labor ended,
    Jordan past."*

6 If I ask Him to receive me,
  Will He say me nay?
"Not till earth, and not till heaven
  Pass away."

7 Finding, following, keeping, struggling
  Is He sure to bless?
"Saints, apostles, prophets, martyrs,
  Answer, Yes!"   AMEN.

131.   7s.   *(Hymnal 449.)*

CHILDREN of the Heavenly King,
  As we journey, sweetly sing;
Sing our Saviour's worthy praise,
Glorious in His works and ways.

2 We are traveling home to God
  In the way the fathers trod:
They are happy now, and we
Soon their happiness shall see.

3 Banished once, by sin betray'd,
  Christ our advocate was made;
Pardon'd now, no more we roam,
Christ conducts us to our home.

4 Lord, obediently we go,
  Gladly leaving all below,
Only Thou our leader be,
And we still will follow Thee.   AMEN.

132. *6s. 5s., double.*

THOSE eternal bowers
  Man hath never trod,
Those unfading flowers,
  Round the throne of God ;
Who may hope to gain them,
  After weary fight ?
Who at length attain them,
  Clad in robes of white ?

2 He, who gladly barters
  All on earthly ground,
He, who like the martyrs,
  Says, "*I will be crowned :*"
He, whose one oblation
  Is a life of love ;
Clinging to the nation
  Of the blest above.

3 Shame upon you, legions
  Of the Heavenly King,
Citizens of regions
  Past imagining !
What ! with pipe and tabor
  Fool away the light !
When He bids you labor,
  When He tells you "*Fight !*"

4 While I do my duty
Struggling through the tide,
Whisper Thou of beauty
On the other side !
Tell who will the story
Of this life's distress ;
O the future glory !
O the loveliness !   AMEN.

133.   *7s. 6s., double.*

STAND up, stand up for Jesus !
Ye soldiers of the cross;
Lift high His royal banner,
It must not suffer loss.
From vict'ry unto vict'ry,
His army shall He lead ;
Till ev'ry foe is vanquished,
And Christ is Lord indeed.

2 Stand up, stand up for Jesus !
Stand in His strength alone ;
The arm of flesh will fail you,
Ye dare not trust your own.
Put on the gospel armor,
And watching unto prayer,
Where duty calls, or danger,
Be never wanting there.

In the march to vict'ry
  Be our toils forgot !
Onward still, and upward !
  Fear not slight nor frown !
Soon in joy and triumph,
  Ye shall wear the crown !—*Chor.*

AMEN.

114. *C. M.* *(Hymnal 471.)*

AM I a soldier of the cross,
  A follower of the Lamb ?
And shall I fear to own His cause,
  Or blush to speak His Name ?

2 Must I be carried to the skies
  On flowery beds of ease,
While others fought to win the prize,
  And sailed through bloody seas ?

3 Are there no foes for me to face ?
  Must I not stem the flood ?
Is the gay world a friend to grace,
  To help me on to God ?

4 Sure I must fight if I would reign ;
  Increase my courage, Lord ;
I 'll bear the cross, endure the pain,
  Supported by Thy word. AMEN.

115.   *S. M.*   *(Hymnal 216.)*

SOLDIERS of Christ, arise,
  And put your armor on,
Strong in the strength which God supplies
  Through His eternal Son.

2 Strong in the Lord of hosts,
  And in His mighty power;
Who in the strength of Jesus trusts,
  Is more than conqueror.

3 Stand then in His great might,
  With all His strength endued;
And take, to arm you for the fight,
  The panoply of God.

4 That having all things done,
  And all your conflicts past,
Ye may behold your victory won,
  And stand complete at last.   AMEN.

116.

SOUND the battle-cry!
  See, the foe is nigh!
Raise the standard high
  For the Lord:
Gird your armor on,
  Stand firm, every one;
Rest your cause upon
  His holy word.

4 A noble army, men and boys,
The matron and the maid,
Around the Saviour's throne rejoice,
In robes of light array'd :
They climbed the dizzy steep of heaven,
Through peril, toil, and pain :
O God ! to us may grace be given
To follow in their train !   AMEN.

136.   6s. 4s.   *(Hymnal 237.)*

MY faith looks up Thee,
Thou Lamb of Calvary,
Saviour divine !
Now hear me while I pray :
Take all my guilt away ;
Oh ! let me from this day
Be wholly Thine.

2 May Thy rich grace impart
Strength to my fainting heart ;
My zeal inspire ;
As Thou hast died for me,
O may my love to Thee
Pure, warm, and changeless be,
A living fire.

3 While life's dark maze I tread,
And griefs around me spread,
Be Thou my guide ;

Bid darkness turn to day ;
Wipe sorrow's tears away,
Nor let me ever stray
From Thee aside.   Amen

137.   *D. C. M.*

I HEARD the voice of Jesus say,
  "Come unto me and rest ;
Lay down, thou weary one, lay down
  Thy head upon My breast."
I came to Jesus, as I was,
  Weary, and worn, and sad ;
I found in Him a resting-place,
  And He has made me glad.

2 I heard the voice of Jesus say,
  "Behold I freely give
The living water; thirsty one,
  Stoop down and drink, and live."
I came to Jesus, and I drank
  Of that life-giving stream ;
My thirst was quenched, my soul revived,
  And now I live in Him.

3 I heard the voice of Jesus say,
  "I am this dark world's light ;
Look unto Me, thy morn shall rise,
  And all thy day be bright."

I looked to Jesus, and I found
In Him my Star, my Sun ;
And in that light of life I 'll walk,
Till traveling days are done.   AMEN.

138.   8s. 7s. 7s.   *(Hymnal 233.)*

ONCE in royal David's city
Stood a lowly cattle shed,
Where a mother laid her Baby,
In a manger for His bed ;
Mary was that mother mild,
Jesus Christ her little Child.

2 He came down to earth from Heaven
Who is God and Lord of all,
And His shelter was a stable,
And His cradle was a stall ;
With the poor, and mean, and lowly,
Lived on earth our Saviour holy.

3 And, thro' all His wondrous childhood,
He would honor and obey,
Love, and watch the lovely maiden
In whose gentle arms He lay ;
Christian children all must be
Mild, obedient, good as He.

4 For He is our childhood's pattern,
Day by day like us He grew ;

He was-little, weak, and helpless,
    Tears and smiles like us He knew ;
And He feeleth for our sadness,
And He shareth in our gladness.

5 And our eyes at last shall see Him,
    Through His own redeeming love,
For that Child so dear and gentle
    Is our Lord in Heaven above ;
And He leads His children on
To the place where He has gone.

6 Not in that poor lowly stable,
    With the oxen standing by,
We shall see Him ; but in heaven,
    Set at God's right hand on high :
When like stars His children crowned
All in white shall wait around.   AMEN.

139.   11s.   *(Hymnal 398.)*

HOW firm a foundation, ye saints of the Lord,
    Is laid for your faith in His excellent word !
What more can He say than to you He hath
        said,
You who unto Jesus for refuge have fled ?

2 Fear not, I am with thee, O be not dismay'd,
I, I am thy God, and will still give thee aid ;

I 'll strengthen thee, help thee, and cause thee
   to stand,
Upheld by My righteous, omnipotent hand.

3 When through the deep waters I call thee
   to go,
The rivers of woe shall not thee overflow ;
For I will be with thee, thy troubles to bless,
And sanctify to thee thy deepest distress.

4 When through fiery trials thy pathway shall lie,
My grace, all-sufficient, shall be thy supply ;
The flame shall not hurt thee ; I only design
Thy dross to consume, and thy gold to refine.

5 The soul that to Jesus hath fled for repose,
I will not, I will not desert to his foes ;
That soul, though all hell shall endeavor to
   shake,
I 'll never—no never—no, never forsake.

Amen.

140.   *S. M.*   *(Hymnal 474)*

A CHARGE to keep I have,
   A God to glorify ;
A never-dying soul to save,
   And fit it for the sky :

2 From youth to hoary age,
   My calling to fulfill :

O may it all my powers engage
  To do my Master's will.

3 Arm me with jealous care,
    As in Thy sight to live,
  And O Thy servant, Lord, prepare
    A strict account to give.

4 Help me to watch and pray,
    And on Thyself rely :
  Assured if I my trust betray,
    I shall for ever die.   AMEN.

141.   7s.

GOD of mercy, thron'd on high,
    Listen from Thy lofty seat ;
  Hear, O hear our feeble cry,
    Guide, O guide our wand'ring feet !

2 Young and erring travelers, we
    All our dangers do not know ;
  Scarcely fear the stormy sea,
    Hardly feel the tempest blow.

3 Jesus, lover of the young,
    Cleanse us with Thy blood divine !
  Ere the tide of sin grow strong,
    Save us, keep us, make us Thine !

4 When perplexed in danger's snare,
    Thou alone our guide canst be ;

When oppress'd with woe and care,
Whom have we to trust but Thee?

5 Let us ever hear Thy voice,
   Ask Thy counsel every day ;
Saints and angels will rejoice,
   If we walk in wisdom's way.   AMEN

142.   8s. 7s. 4.

LORD, I hear of show'rs of blessing
   Thou art scattering full and free ;
Show'rs the thirsty land refreshing :
   Let some droppings fall on me !
   ‖: Even me, :‖
Let some droppings fall on me !

2 Pass me not, O God, my Father !
   Sinful though my heart may be ;
Thou might'st leave me, but the rather
   Let Thy mercy fall on me !
   ‖: Even me, :‖
Let Thy mercy fall on me !

3 Pass me not, O gracious Saviour !
   Let me live and cling to Thee :
For I'm longing for Thy favor ;
   Whilst Thou 'rt calling, O call me !
   ‖: Even me, :‖
Whilst Thou 'rt calling, O call me !

4 Pass me not, O mighty Spirit!
    Thou canst make the blind to see-
Witnesser of Jesu's merit,
    Speak the word of power to me!
        ‖: Even me, :‖
Speak the word of power to me!

5 Pass me not! Thy lost one bringing;
    Bind my heart, O Lord, to Thee;
Whilst the streams of life are springing,
    Blessing others, O bless me!
        ‖: Even me, :‖
Blessing others, O bless me!   AMEN.

HEAVEN.

143.   *(Hymnal 485.)*

HARK! hark, my soul!   Angelic songs are
        swelling
    O'er earth's green fields, and ocean's wave-
        beat shore:
How sweet the truth those blessèd strains are
        telling
Of that new life when sin shall be no more.

    Chorus.—Angels of Jesus,
            Angels of light,
            Singing to welcome
                The pilgrims of the night.

151

2 Onward we go, for still we hear them singing,
　　"*Come, weary souls, for Jesus bids you come :*"
　　And, through the dark its echoes sweetly ring-
　　　　ing,
　　The music of the Gospel leads us home.
—Chor.

3 Far, far away, like bells at evening pealing,
　　The voice of Jesus sounds o'er land and sea ;
　　And laden souls by thousands meekly steal-
　　　　ing,
　　Kind Shepherd, turn their weary steps to
　　　　Thee.—*Chor.*

4 Rest comes at length, though life be long and
　　　　dreary,
　　The day must dawn, and darksome night be
　　　　past ;
　　All journeys end in welcome to the weary,
　　And Heaven, the heart's true home, will come
　　　　at last.—*Chor.*

5 Angels, sing on ! your faithful watches keep-
　　　　ing ;
　　Sing us sweet fragments of the songs above ;
　　Till morning's joy shall end the night of weep-
　　　　ing,
　　And life's long shadows break in cloudless
　　　　love.—*Chor.*　　　　　　　　Amen.

152

144.   *7s. 6s., double.*

BRIEF life is here our portion,
   Brief sorrow, short-lived care ;
The life that knows no ending,
   The tearless life is there.
O happy retribution !
   Short toil, eternal rest ;
For mortals and for sinners,
   A mansion with the blest.

2 And now we fight the battle,
   But then shall wear the crown
Of full, and everlasting,
   And passionless renown.
But He Whom now we trust in
   Shall then be seen and known ;
And they that know and see Him
   Shall have Him for their own.

3 The morning shall awaken,
   The shadow shall decay,
And each true-hearted servant
   Shall shine as doth the day ;
There God, our King and portion,
   In fullness of His grace,
Shall we behold for ever,
   And worship face to face.

4 O sweet and blessèd country,
  The Home of God's elect !
O sweet and blessèd country
  That eager hearts expect !
Jesu, in mercy bring us
  To that dear land of rest ;
Who art with God the Father,
  And Spirit, ever blest.   AMEN.

145.   *7s. 6s., double.*   *(Hymnal 493.)*

JERUSALEM the golden !
  With milk and honey blest ;
Beneath thy contemplation
  Sink heart and voice opprest.
I know not, O I know not
  What joys await us there ;
What radiancy of glory,
  What bliss beyond compare.

2 They stand, those halls of Zion,
  All jubilant with song,
And bright with many an angel,
  And all the martyr throng.
The Prince is ever in them,
  The daylight is serene ;
The pastures of the blessèd
  Are decked in glorious sheen.

3 There is the throne of David ;
    And there, from care released,
The shout of them that triumph,
    The song of them that feast ;
And they, who with their Leader
    Have conquered in the fight,
For ever and for ever
    Are clad in robes of white.

4 O sweet and blessèd country,
    The home of God's elect !
O sweet and blessèd country,
    That eager hearts expect !
Jesu, in mercy bring us
    To that dear land of rest ;
Who art with God the Father,
    And Spirit, ever blest.   AMEN.

146.   *C. M., with chorus.*

COME Lord, and warm each languid heart,
    Inspire each lifeless tongue ;
And let the joys of Heaven impart
    Their influence to our song.

Chorus.

They'll sing their welcome home to us :
They'll sing their welcome home to us :
    The angels will stand
    On the Heavenly strand,

And sing their welcome home.
Welcome home!   Welcome home!
    The angels will stand
    On the Heavenly strand,
And sing their welcome home.

2 Sorrow and pain, and every care,
    And discord there shall cease:
And perfect joy, and love sincere
    Adorn the realms of peace.—*Chor.*

3 There on a throne (how dazzling bright!)
    Th' exalted Saviour shines,
And beams ineffable delight
    On all the heavenly minds.—*Chor.*

4 There shall the followers of the Lamb
    Join in immortal songs;
And endless honors to His Name
    Employ their tuneful tongues.—*Chor.*

5 Lord, tune our hearts to praise and love,
    Our feeble notes inspire;
Till in Thy blissful courts above,
    We join th' angelic choir.—*Chor.*   AMEN.

147.   *S. M., with chorus.*   *(Hymnal 462.)*
COME we that love the Lord,
    And let our joys be known;

Join in a song with sweet accord,
  And thus surround the throne.

Chorus.

We'll be there! We'll be there!
Palms of victory, crowns of glory we shall wear;
In that beautiful world on high.

2 Let those refuse to sing
    That never knew our God,
  But children of the Heavenly King
    May speak their joys abroad.—*Chor.*

3 The God of Heaven is ours,
    Our Father and our love ;
  He shall send down His heavenly powers
    To carry us above.—*Chor.*

4 There shall we see His face,
    And never, never sin ;
  There, from the rivers of His grace,
    Drink endless pleasures in.—*Chor.*

5 Then let our songs abound,
    And every tear be dry ;
  We're marching through Emmanuel's ground,
    To fairer worlds on high.—*Chor.*   AMEN.

148.   *(Hymnal 509.)*

O PARADISE, O Paradise,
    O Land of perfect rest !

Who would not seek the happy land
Where they that loved are blest?
Chorus.—Where loyal hearts and true
Stand ever in the light,
All rapture through and through,
In God's most holy sight.

2 O Paradise, O Paradise,
I want to sin no more,
I want to be as pure on earth
As on thy spotless shore:—*Chor.*

3 Lord Jesus, King of Paradise,
O keep me in Thy love,
And guide me to that happy land
Of perfect rest above:—*Chor.*   AMEN.

149.

BEAUTIFUL mansions, Home of the blest,
Land where the faithful, Ever shall rest;
There is my treasure, There shall I be;
Saviour in Heaven, Lead me to Thee.

Chorus.—Saviour, be near me,
Thy gentle voice can cheer me,
O Jesus my Saviour,
Lead me to Thee.

2 Here in a desert, Cheerless I roam,
Laden with sorrow, Far from my home;

Clouds on my pathway, Darkly I see,
Saviour in Heaven, Lead me to Thee.—*Chor.*

3 Thou wilt not leave me, Comfortless here,
Why should I doubt Thee? What do I fear?
Light in the distance, Breaking I see,
Saviour in Heaven, Lead me to Thee.—*Chor.*

4 Jesus, I love Thee, Dwell in my heart,
Never, O never, From me depart;
Hope like a rainbow, Shining I see,
Saviour in Heaven, I'll be with Thee.—*Chor.*

AMEN.

150.   *8s. 7s., double, with chorus.*

THERE'S a home of joy unfading,
  Let us seek it, 't is not far;
There's a Saviour's love unchanging,
  Just within the gates ajar.
Enter in and share His glory,
  Loving arms will fold us there,
We'll behold the heavenly mansions
  Just within the gates ajar.

Chorus.—Hark! the music softly stealing
      From the angel choir afar!
      They are singing, sweetly singing;—
      Enter in,—the gate's ajar.

2 No more weeping, no more sadness,
  No more strife, nor anxious care;

List ! the heavenly songs of gladness
　Stealing through the gates ajar !
No more longings, no more pinings,
　Wing their way thro' midnight air,
Hark ! the voice of mercy calling
　Thro' the heavenly gates ajar !—*Chor.*

3 'T is a loving Saviour calls us,
　Bids us all His glories share ;
Crowns of life He 'll surely give us
　When within the gates ajar.
Look to Jesus—trust His mercy—
　Look to Him by faith and prayer,—
Live for Jesus—precious Saviour,—
　Opening wide the gates ajar.—*Chor.*

4 Soon we 'll reach the heavenly portals,
　Angel bands will hail us there,
Then we 'll catch the strains immortal,
　Bursting through the gates ajar.
Saviour, give us hearts to love Thee,
　Guide us to that land afar,
Through the shades of death's dark valley,
　May we see the gates ajar.—*Chor.*　Amen.

151.　　　11s., *with chorus.*

IN the far better land of glory and light
　The ransomed are singing in garments of
　　white,

The harpers are harping, and all the bright
    train
Sing the song of redemption—"*The Lamb that
    was slain.*"

Chorus.

Hallelujah to the Lamb! Hallelujah to the Lamb!
Hallelujah! Hallelujah! Hallelujah! Amen.

2 Like the sound of the sea swells their chorus
    of praise
  Round the star-circled crown of the Ancient
    of days,
  And the thrones and dominions re-echo the
    strain
  Of the glory eternal to Him that was slain.
—*Chor.*

3 Dear Saviour, may we, with our voices so faint,
  Sing the chorus enrapturing with angel and
    saint?
  Yes, yes, we will sing, and Thine ear we will
    gain
  With the song of redemption—"*The Lamb that
    was slain.—Chor.* AMEN

X.—SPECIAL SEASONS AND SERVICES.

MORNING.

152. *L. M.* *(Hymnal 332.)*

ALL praise to Thee, who safe hast kept,
And hast refresh'd me while I slept:
Grant, Lord, when I from death shall wake,
I may of endless life partake.

2 Lord, I my vows to Thee renew;
Scatter my sins as morning dew;
Guard my first springs of thought and will,
And with Thyself my spirit fill.

3 Direct, control, suggest this day,
All I design, or do, or say,
That all my powers, with all their might,
In Thy sole glory may unite.

4 Praise God, from Whom all blessings flow;
Praise Him, all creatures here below;
Praise Him above, ye heavenly host;
Praise Father, Son, and Holy Ghost.   AMEN

EVENING.

153. *L. M.* *(Hymnal 336.)*

SUN of my soul, Thou Saviour dear,
It is not night if Thou be near;

O may no earth-born cloud arise
To hide Thee from Thy servant's eyes.

2 When the soft dews of kindly sleep
My wearied eyelids gently steep,
Be my last thought, How sweet to rest
For ever on my Saviour's breast!

3 Abide with me from morn till eve,
For without Thee I cannot live ;
Abide with me when night is nigh,
For without Thee I dare not die.

4 If some poor wandering child of Thine
Have spurn'd to-day the voice divine,
Now, Lord, the gracious work begin ;
Let him no more lie down in sin.

5 Watch by the sick ; enrich the poor
With blessings from Thy boundless store ;
Be every mourner's sleep to-night,
Like infants' slumbers, pure and bright.

6 Come near and bless us when we wake,
Ere through the world our way we take ;
Till in the ocean of Thy love
We lose ourselves in Heaven above. AMEN.

154.   **10s.**   *(Hymnal 335.)*

ABIDE with me : fast falls the eventide ;
The darkness deepens ; Lord, with me
  abide ;
When other helpers fail, and comforts flee,
Help of the helpless, O abide with me.

2 Swift to its close ebbs out life's little day ;
Earth's joys grow dim, its glories pass away ;
Change and decay in all around I see :
O Thou who changest not, abide with me.

3 I need Thy presence every passing hour ;
What but Thy grace can foil the tempter's
  power ?
Who like Thyself my guide and stay can be ?
Through cloud and sunshine, O abide with me.

4 I fear no foe with Thee at hand to bless ;
Ills have no weight, and tears no bitterness :
Where is death's sting ? where, grave, thy vic-
  tory ?
I triumph still, if Thou abide with me.

5 Hold Thou Thy cross before my closing eyes ;
Shine through the gloom, and point me to the
  skies ;

Heaven's morning breaks, and earth's vain
   shadows flee :
In life, in death, O Lord, abide with me.
                          Amen.

155.   7s.   *(Hymnal 340.)*

SOFTLY now the light of day
   Fades upon my sight away ;
Free from care, from labor free,
   Lord, I would commune with Thee:

2 Thou, whose all-pervading eye,
   Nought escapes, without, within,
Pardon each infirmity,
   Open fault, and secret sin.

3 Soon, for me, the light of day
   Shall forever pass away ;
Then, from sin and sorrow free,
   Take me, Lord, to dwell with Thee:

4 Thou, who, sinless, yet hast known
   All of man's infirmity ;
Then, from Thine eternal throne,
   Jesus, look with pitying eye.   Amen.

156.   *L. M.*   *(Hymnal 333.)*

ALL praise to Thee, my God, this night,
   For all the blessings of the light:

Keep me, O keep me, King of kings,
Under Thine own Almighty wings.

2 Forgive me, Lord, for Thy dear Son,
The ills that I this day have done ;
That with the world, myself, and Thee,
I, ere I sleep, at peace may be.

3 Teach me to live, that I may dread
The grave as little as my bed ;
Teach me to die, that so I may
Triumphing rise at the last day.

4 O may my soul on Thee repose,
And with sweet sleep mine eyelids close :
Sleep, that may me more vigorous make
To serve my God, when I awake.

5 Praise God, from Whom all blessings flow;
Praise Him, all creatures here below ;
Praise Him above, ye heavenly host ;
Praise Father, Son, and Holy Ghost. AMEN.

MISSIONS.

157. 6s. 4s. *(Hymnal 146.)*

THOU, Whose Almighty word
Chaos and darkness heard,
And took their flight ;

Hear us, we humbly pray;
And where the Gospel-day
Sheds not its glorious ray,
Let there be light!

2 Thou, Who didst come to bring,
On Thy redeeming wing,
Healing and sight,
Health to the sick in mind,
Sight to the inly blind,
O now to all mankind
Let there be light!

3 Spirit of truth and love,
Life-giving, holy Dove!
Speed forth Thy flight!
Move on the water's face,
Bearing the lamp of grace,
And in earth's darkest place
Let there be light!   AMEN.

158.   *L. M.*

FLING out the banner! Let it float
Skyward and seaward, high and wide;
The sun, that lights its shining folds,
The cross, on which the Saviour died.

2 Fling out the banner! Angels bend
In anxious silence o'er the sign;

And vainly seek to comprehend
  The wonder of the love divine.

3 Fling out the banner! Heathen lands
    Shall see from far the glorious sight,
  And nations, crowding to be born,
    Baptize their spirits in its light.

4 Fling out the banner! Sin-sick souls
    That sink and perish in the strife,
  Shall touch in faith its radiant hem,
    And spring immortal into life.

5 Fling out the banner! Let it float
    Skyward and seaward, high and wide,
  Our glory, only in the cross;
    Our only hope, the Crucified!   AMEN.

159.   *8s. 7s., double.*

LORD, our offerings we are bringing,
    Smile upon them from above;
  And while we Thy praise are singing,
    O regard us with Thy love.
  Take, we pray Thee, our oblation.
    Which we bring in Jesus' name;
  That the news of Thy salvation
    We may thus to men proclaim.

2 There is in it nought of merit,
    To commend it to Thy care,

And we therefore humbly bear it
　To Thy throne in earnest prayer.
Let Thy blessing, Lord, attend it,
　As the sun matures the grain ;
For if Thou shouldst not befriend it,
　All our work will be in vain.

3 We would tell to distant nations,
　All the story of Thy love ;
And the riches of salvation,
　We would have them freely prove.
From the gifts our hands have brought Thee,
　May it, Lord, at last appear,
Some benighted souls have sought Thee,
　And, like us, have found Thee near.

4 Speed Thy cause, Thou bless'd Saviour,
　Hasten on that glorious day,
When from earth's remotest regions
　Sin's dark clouds shall pass away :
Hear the cry we breathe before Thee,
　Answer from Thy throne above,
Let the nations see Thy glory,
　Bless the peoples with Thy love.　　Amen

160.　　　　　　　7s. 6s., *double.*

THE morning light is breaking,
　The darkness disappears ;

The sons of earth are waking
    To penitential tears :
Each breeze that sweeps the ocean
    Brings tidings from afar
Of nations in commotion
    Prepared for Zion's war.

2 Rich dews of grace come o'er us,
    In many a gentle shower,
And brighter scenes before us
    Are opening every hour :
Each cry to heaven going
    Abundant answer brings,
And heavenly gales are blowing
    With peace upon their wings.

3 See heathen nations bending
    Before the God of love,
And thousand hearts ascending
    In gratitude above :
While sinners, now confessing,
    The gospel's call obey,
And seek a Saviour's blessing,
    A nation in a day.   AMEN

161.   7s. 6s., *double.*   *(Hymnal 283.)*

FROM Greenland's icy mountains,
    From India's coral strand,

Where Afric's sunny fountains
  Roll down their golden sand ;
From many an ancient river,
  From many a palmy plain,
They call us to deliver
  Their land from error's chain.

2 What though the spicy breezes
  Blow soft o'er Ceylon's Isle ;
Though every prospect pleases,
  And only man is vile :
In vain with lavish kindness
  The gifts of God are strewn :
The heathen in his blindness
  Bows down to wood and stone.

3 Shall we, whose souls are lighted
  With wisdom from on high ;
Shall we to men benighted
  The lamp of life deny ?
Salvation, O salvation,
  The joyful sound proclaim,
Till each remotest nation
  Has learnt Messiah's Name.

4 Waft, waft, ye winds, His story,
  And you, ye waters, roll,
Till, like a sea of glory,
  It spreads from pole to pole :

Till o'er our ransom'd nature,
The Lamb for sinners slain,
Redeemer, King, Creator,
In bliss returns to reign.   AMEN.

162.   *L. M.*   *(Hymnal 284.)*

JESUS shall reign where'er the sun
Does his successive journeys run;
His kingdom stretch from shore to shore,
Till moons shall wax and wane no more.

2 To Him shall endless prayer be made,
And praises throng to crown His head;
His Name like sweet perfume shall rise
With every morning sacrifice.

3 People and realms, of every tongue,
Dwell on His love with sweetest song;
And infant voices shall proclaim
Their early blessings on His Name.

4 Blessings abound where'er He reigns;
The prisoner leaps to burst his chains,
The weary find eternal rest,
And all the sons of want are blest.

5 Let every creature rise, and bring,
Peculiar honors to our King:
Angels descend with songs again,
And earth repeat the loud Amen.   AMEN

163. **FUNERALS.**

PEACEFULLY lay *her* down to rest,
Place the turf kindly on her breast ;
Sweet is the slumber beneath the sod,
While the pure soul is resting with God.

Chorus.

Peacefully sleep,—Peacefully sleep,
Sleep till that morning,—Peacefully sleep.

2 Close to *her* lone and narrow house,
Gracefully wave, ye willow boughs ;
Flowers of the wild-wood your odor shed
Over the holy, beautiful dead.—*Chor.*

3 Quietly sleep, belovèd one,
Rest from thy toil—thy labor done ;
Rest till the trump from the opening skies
Bid thee from dust to glory arise !—*Chor.*

AMEN.

164. *L. M.* *(Hymnal 260.)*

ASLEEP in Jesus ! blessèd sleep !
From which none ever wakes to weep ;
A calm and undisturbed repose,
Unbroken by the last of foes.

2 Asleep in Jesus ! oh, how sweet,
To be for such a slumber meet ;
With holy confidence to sing
That death has lost its painful sting !

3 Asleep in Jesus ! peaceful rest !
Whose waking is supremely blest ;
No fear, no woe shall dim that hour
That manifests the Saviour's power.

4 Asleep in Jesus ! O for me
May such a blissful refuge be ;
Securely shall my ashes lie,
Waiting the summons from on high.

5 Asleep in Jesus ! far from thee
Thy kindred and their graves may be ;
But there is still a blessèd sleep,
From which none ever wakes to weep.

AMEN.

XI.—MISCELLANEOUS HYMNS.

165.   *6s. 5s., double.*

BRIGHTLY gleams our banner,
    Pointing to the sky,
Waving wand'rers onward
    To their home on high.
Journeying to our Heaven,
    Gladly thus we pray,
And, with hearts united,
    Take our upward way.
Chorus.—Brightly gleams our banner,
    Pointing to the sky,

Waving wand'rers onward
To their home on high.

2 Hail ! sweet Jesus, Master,
  Round Thy sacred feet,
Here, with hearts rejoicing,
  See Thy children meet.
Oft, alas ! we leave Thee,
  Straying far away,
Now once more we'll enter
  On the narrow way.—*Chor.*

3 All our days direct us,—
  Make us meek and mild,
By Thy Childhood's pattern,—
  Mary's holy Child.
Bid Thine angels shield us,
  When the storm-clouds lower,
Pardon Thou—protect us
  At death's solemn hour.

4 Jesu ! Saints and angels
  With Thy church combine,
Offering prayers and praises
  At Thy glorious shrine :
When the toil is over,
  Then comes rest and peace,
Jesus in His beauty,—
  Songs that never cease.—*Chor.*   AMEN

166.   6s. 5s., *double.*   *(Hymnal 232.)*

ONWARD, Christian soldiers,
  Marching as to war,
With the cross of Jesus
  Going on before :
Christ, the royal Master,
  Leads against the foe ;
Forward into battle,
  See, His banners go.

Chorus.—Onward, Christian soldiers,
  Marching as to war,
  With the cross of Jesus
  Going on before.

2 At the sign of triumph,
    Satan's host doth flee,
  On, then, Christian soldiers,
    On to victory.
  Hell's foundations quiver,
    At the shout of praise ;
  Brothers, lift your voices,
    Loud your anthems raise.—*Chor.*

3 Like a mighty army,
    Moves the church of God,
  Brothers, we are treading
    Where the saints have trod

We are not divided,
   All one body we,
One in hope, in doctrine,
   One in charity.—*Chor.*

4 Crowns and thrones may perish,
   Kingdoms rise and wane,
But the church of Jesus
   Constant will remain ;
Gates of hell can never
   'Gainst that church prevail ;
We have Christ's own promise,
   And that cannot fai .—*Chor.*

5 Onward, then, ye people,
   Join our happy throng.
Blend with ours your voices.
   In the triumph-song ;
Glory, laud, and honor.
   Unto Christ the King,
This through countless ages,
   Men and angels sing.—*Chor.*   AMEN

167.

MARCHING on ! Marching on ! glad as
      birds on the wing,
   Come the bright ranks of children from near
      and from far ;

Happy hearts, full of song, 'neath our banners
    we bring,
  Little soldiers of Zion prepare for the
    war.

Chorus.

Marching on ! Marching on ! sound the battle-
  cry, sound the battle-cry.
For the Saviour is before us, and for Him we
  draw the sword.
Marching on ! Marching on ! shout the victory,
  shout the victory !
We will end our battle, singing, " *Hallelujah
  to the Lord !* "

2 Pressing on ! Pressing on ! to the din of the
    fray,
  With the firm tread of faith to the battle we
    go ;
  'Mid the cheering of angels, our ranks march
    away,
  With our flags pointing ever right on toward
    the foe.—*Chor.*

3 Fighting on ! Fighting on ! in the midst of
    the strife,
  At the call of our Captain we draw every
    sword,

We are battling for God, we are struggling for
    life,
  Let us strike every rebel that fights 'gainst
    the Lord.—*Chor.*

4 Singing on!   Singing on! from the battle we
    come,
  Every flag bears a wreath, every soldier re-
    nown ;
  Heavenly angels are waiting to welcome us
    home,
  And the Saviour will give us a robe and a
    crown.—*Chor.*   Amen.

168.

COME with singing—
  Gladly bringing
Songs of praise to Christ our King
  Lord, be near us,
  Kindly hear us,
While our grateful notes we sing.

Chorus.

Bless us, save us ;
Jesus, show thy precious love ;
Hark ! hark ! our Saviour tells us,
  Come ! come ! come ! come !

2   Tell the story
     Of the glory
  Of our ever-blessèd Lord ;
     Love abounding,
     Sin confounding,—
  Tell His goodness all abroad

     Chorus.

  Guide us, lead us,
  To Thy blessed Heaven above.
  Hark ! hark ! He freely calls us
    Home ! home ! home ! home !

3   He, to save us,
     Freely gave us
  All He had, in boundless love ;
     We, believing,
     Grace receiving,
  Hope, thro' Him, for Heaven above.
    Chor.—Guide us, etc.   Amen

169.   6s. 4s.

M Y country ! 't is of thee,
  Sweet land of liberty !
   Of thee I sing.
 Land where my fathers died ;
 Land of the pilgrim's pride ;
 From ev'ry mountain side
   Let freedom ring !

2 My native country! thee,
  Land of the noble free,
    Thy name I love ;
I love thy rocks and rills,
Thy woods and templed hills ;
My heart with rapture thrills,
    Like that above.

3 Our Father's God ! to Thee,
  Author of liberty !
    To Thee we sing ;
Long may our land be bright,
With freedom's holy light,
Protect us by Thy might,
    Great God, our King!   Amen.

170.   *C. M.*   *(Hymnal 163)*.

MY God, how wonderful Thou art,
  Thy majesty how bright,
How beautiful Thy mercy-seat
  In depths of burning light !

2 How wonderful, how beautiful,
  The sight of Thee must be ;
Thine endless wisdom, boundless power,
  And awful purity !

3 O how I fear Thee, Living God,
  With deepest, tenderest fears ;

And worship Thee with trembling hope,
And penitential tears !

4 Yet I may love Thee, too, O Lord,
Almighty as Thou art,
For Thou hast stooped to ask of me
The love of my poor heart.   AMEN.

171.

THE Shadow of the Rock !
Stay, pilgrim, stay !
Night treads upon the heels of day,
There is no other resting-place this way.
The Rock is near,
The well is clear.
‖: Rest in the Shadow of the Rock ! :‖

2   The Shadow of the Rock !
To weary feet,
That have been diligent and fleet,
The sleep is deeper, and the shade more sweet,
O weary, rest !
Thou art sore pressed—
‖: Rest in the Shadow of the Rock ! :‖

3   The Shadow of the Rock !
One day of pain,
Thou scarce wilt hope the Rock to gain,
Yet there wilt sleep thy last sleep on the plain ;

And only wake
In Heaven's daybreak—
|: Rest in the Shadow of the Rock ! :| Amen.

172.

THERE is beauty all around,
    When there's love at home ;
There is joy in every sound,
    When there's love at home.
Peace and plenty here abide,
    Smiling sweet on every side,
Time doth softly, sweetly glide,
    When there's love at home.
Chorus.—Love at home, love at home ;
        Time doth softly, sweetly glide,
        When there's love at home.

2 In the cottage there is joy,
    When there's love at home ;
Hate and envy ne'er annoy,
    When there's love at home.
Roses blossom 'neath our feet,
    All the earth's a garden sweet,
Making life a bliss complete,
    When there's love at home.
Chorus.—Love at home, love at home ;
        Making life a bliss complete,
        When there's love at home.

3 Kindly heaven smiles above,
   When there 's love at home ;
All the earth is filled with love,
   When there 's love at home.
Sweeter sings the brooklet by,
   Brighter beams the azure sky ;
O there 's One who smiles on high
   When there 's love at home.
Chorus.—Love at home, love at home ;
     O there 's One who smiles on high
     When there 's love at home.

4 Jesus, make me wholly Thine,
   Then there 's love at home ;
May Thy sacrifice be mine,
   Then there 's love at home.
Safely from all harm I 'll rest,
   With no sinful care distressed
Thro' Thy tender mercy blessed,
   With Thy love at home.
Chorus.—Love at home, love at home ;
     Thro' Thy tender mercy blessed,
     With Thy love at home.   Amen

173.   *L. M.*   *(Hymnal 409.,*

BEFORE Jehovah's awful throne,
   Ye nations, bow with sacred joy ;
Know that the Lord is God alone ;
He can create, and He destroy.

2 His sovereign power, without our aid,
  Made us of clay, and form'd us men ;
And when like wandering sheep we stray'd,
  He brought us to His fold again.

3 We 'll crowd Thy gates with thankful songs,
  High as the heaven our voices raise ;
And earth, with her ten thousand tongues,
  Shall fill Thy courts with sounding praise.

4 Wide as the world is Thy command,
  Vast as eternity Thy love !
Firm as a rock Thy truth must stand,
  When rolling years shall cease to move.

AMEN.

XII.—INFANT HYMNS.

174.   6s. 5s.

JESUS, gentlest Saviour !
    God of might and power !
Thou Thyself art dwelling
    In us at this hour.

2 Nature cannot hold Thee,
    Heaven is all too straight
For Thine endless glory,
    And Thy royal state.

3 Out beyond the shining
    Of the furthest star,

Thou art ever reaching
  Infinitely far.

4 Yet the hearts of children
    Hold what worlds can not,
  And the God of wonders
    Loves the lowly spot.

5 Jesus, gentlest Saviour !
    Thou art in us now ;
  Fill us full of goodness
    Till our hearts o'erflow.   AMEN.

175.   *8s. 7s., double.*

LITTLE children, Come to Jesus,
    Hear Him saying, Come to me ;
Blessèd Jesus, Who to save us,
    Shed His blood on Calvary.
Little souls were made to serve Him ;
    All His holy law fulfill :
Little hearts were made to love Him ;
    Little hands to do His will.

2 Little eyes to read the Bible,
    Given from the heavens above ;
  Little ears to hear the story
    Of the Saviour's wondrous love ;
  Little tongues to sing His praises ;
    Little feet to walk His ways ;

Little bodies to be temples
  Where the Holy Spirit stays.   Amen.

176.

JESUS, dear, I come to Thee,
  Thou hast said I may ;
Tell me what my life should be,
  Take my sins away.
Jesus, dear, I learn of Thee,
  In Thy word divine,
Every promise there I see,
  May I call it mine.

Chorus.—Jesus, hear my humble song,
     I am weak, but Thou art strong ;
     Gently lead my soul along,
     Help me come to Thee.

2 Jesus, dear, I long for Thee,
  Long Thy peace to know,
Grant those purer joys to me,
  Earth can ne'er bestow.
Jesus, dear, I cling to Thee ;
  When my heart is sad,
Thou wilt kindly speak to me,
  Thou wilt make me glad.—*Chor.*

3 Jesus, dear, I trust in Thee,
  Trust Thy tender love,

There 's a happy home for me,
    With Thy saints above;
Jesus, I would come to Thee,
    Thou hast said I may,
Tell me what my life should be,
    Take my sins away.—*Chor.*   AMEN.

177.   *8s. 6s., double.*

DEAR Saviour, ever at my side !.
    How loving Thou must be,
To leave Thy home in heaven to guard
    A little child like me !
Thy beautiful and shining face
    I see not tho' so near;
The sweetness of Thy soft, low voice,
    I am too deaf to hear.

2 I cannot feel Thee touch my hand,
    With pressure light and mild,
To check me as my mother does,
    When I 'm a wilful child;
But I have felt Thee in my thoughts,
    Fighting with sin for me;
And when my heart loves God, I know
    The sweetness is from Thee.

3 And when, dear Saviour, I kneel down,
    Morning and night to prayer,

Something there is within my heart,
   Which tells me Thou art there.
Yes, when I pray, Thou prayest, too—
   Thy prayer is all for me,
But when I sleep, Thou sleepest not,
   But watchest patiently.   AMEN.

178.   *6s. 5s.*

DO no sinful action,
   Speak no angry word,
Ye belong to Jesus,
   Children of the Lord.

2 Christ is kind and gentle,
   Christ is pure and true,
And His little children
   Must be holy too.

3 There's a wicked spirit
   Watching round you still,
And he tries to tempt you
   To all harm and ill.

4 But ye must not hear him,
   Though 't is hard for you
To resist the evil
   And the good to do.   AMEN.

179.

BEAUTIFUL faces they that wear
The light of a pleasant spirit there ;
It matters little if dark or fair.

2 Beautiful hands are they that do
The work of the noble, good, and true,
For then so busy the long day through.

3 Beautiful feet are they that go
So swiftly to lighten others' woe,
Through summer's heat or winter's snow.

4 Beautiful children, rich or poor,
Who walk in the pathways, sweet and pure,
That lead to mansions both strong and sure.

AMEN.

180.　　　*6s. 5s., double.*

JESUS, tender Saviour,
Hast Thou died for me ?
Make me very thankful
In my heart to Thee.
When the sad, sad story
Of Thy grief I read,
Make me very sorry,
For my sins, indeed.

2 Now I know Thou lovest
And dost plead for me,

Make me very thankful
In my prayers to Thee.
Soon I hope in glory
At Thy side to stand ;
Make me fit to meet Thee
In that happy land.   AMEN

181.

OH ! what can little hands do
To please the King of heaven ?
The little hands some work may try
To help the poor in misery—
Such grace to mine be given.

2   Oh ! what can little lips do
To please the King of heaven ?
The little lips can praise and pray,
And gentle words of kindness say—
Such grace to mine be given.

3   Oh ! what can little eyes do
To please the King of heaven ?
The little eyes can upward look,
Can learn to read God's holy book—
Such grace to mine be given.

4   Oh ! what can little hearts do
To please the King of heaven ?
The hearts, if God His Spirit send,
Can love and trust the children's Friend—
Such grace to mine be given.

When hearts, and hands, and lips unite
To please the King of heaven.
And serve the Saviour with delight,
They are most precious in His sight—
Such grace to mine be given.   AMEN.

82.

THOU art my Shepherd,
    Caring in every need
Thy little lambs to feed ;
    Trusting Thee still ;
In the green pastures low,
Where living waters flow,
Safe by Thy side I go,
    Fearing no ill.

2 Or, if my way lie
Where death, o'erhanging nigh,
My soul would terrify
    With sudden chill ;—
Yet I am not afraid ;
While softly on my head
Thy tender hand is laid,
    I fear no ill.   AMEN.

83.   *Six 7s.*

THOU that once, on mother's knee,
    Wert a little one like me,

When I wake or go to bed,
Lay Thy hands about my head ;
Let me feel Thee very near,
Jesus Christ, our Saviour dear

2 Be beside me in the light,
Close by me through all the night ;
Make me gentle, kind and true,
Do what mother bids me do ;
Help and cheer me when I fret,
And forgive when I forget.

3 Once wert Thou in cradle laid,
Baby bright, in manger-shade,
With the oxen and the cows,
And the lambs outside the house :
Now Thou art above the sky ;
Canst Thou hear Thy children cry ?

4 Thou art nearer when we pray,
Since Thou art so far away ;
Thou my little hymn wilt hear,
Jesus Christ, our Saviour dear,
Thou that once on mother's knee,
Wert a little one like me.   Amen.

184.   6s. 8s.

WHEN little Samuel woke,
       And heard his Maker's voice,

At every word He spoke
   How much did he rejoice !
O blessed, happy child, to find
The God of heaven so near and kind !

2   If God would speak to me,
   And say He was my Friend,
How happy I should be !
   O how would I attend !
The smallest sin I then should fear,
If God Almighty were so near.

3   And does He never speak ?
   O yes, for, in His word,
He bids me come and seek
   The God that Samuel heard :
In almost every page I see,
The God of Samuel calls to me.

4   And I beneath His care
   May safely rest my head ;
I know that God is there
   To guard my humble bed.
And every sin I well may fear,
Since God Almighty is so near.   AMEN.

185.   *C. M.*   *(Hymnal 231.)*

THERE is a green hill far away,
   Without a city wall,

Where the dear Lord was crucified,
  Who died to save us all.

2 We may not know, we cannot tell,
  What pains He had to bear,
But we believe it was for us
  He hung and suffered there.

3 He died that we might be forgiven,
  He died to make us good,
That we might go at last to heaven,
  Saved by His precious blood.

4 O dearly, dearly has He loved,
  And we must love Him, too,
And trust in His redeeming blood,
  And try His works to do.   Amen.

186.   *(Hymnal 226.)*

I THINK when I read that sweet story of old,
  When Jesus was here among men,
How He call'd little children as lambs to His
    fold,
I should like to have been with them then.

2 I wish that His hands had been placed on my
    head,
That His arm had been thrown around me,
And that I might have seen His kind look
    when He said,
"Let the little ones come unto Me."

3 Yet still to His footstool in prayer I may go,
  And ask for a share in His love ;
And if I thus earnestly seek Him below,
  I shall see Him and hear Him above,

4 In that beautiful place He has gone to prepare
  For all who are wash'd and forgiven ;
And many dear children shall be with him
    there,
  " For such is the kingdom of heaven."

5 But thousands and thousands who wander and
    fall,
  Never heard of that heavenly home ;
I wish they could know there is room for them
    all,
  And that Jesus has bid them to come.

AMEN.

XIII.—DISMISSAL AND DOXOLOGIES.

187.   *L. M.*   *(Hymnal 166.)*

ALMIGHTY Father, bless the word,
  Which through Thy grace, we now have
    heard ;
O may the precious seed take root,
Spring up, and bear abundant fruit.

196

2 We praise Thee for the means of grace,
  Thus in thy courts to seek Thy face,
  Grant, Lord, that we who worship here
  May all, at length, in heaven appear.   AMEN

188.   8s. 7s. 4.   *(Hymnal 165.)*

LORD, dismiss us with Thy blessing,
    Fill our hearts with joy and peace ;
  Let us each, Thy love possessing,
    Triumph in redeeming grace ;
      ||; O refresh us. :||
  Traveling through this wilderness.

2 Thanks we give, and adoration,
    For Thy Gospel's joyful sound ;
  May the fruits of Thy salvation
    In our hearts and lives abound :
      ||: May Thy presence :||
  With us evermore be found.   AMEN.

189.   10s.   *(Hymnal 169.)*

SAVIOUR, again to Thy dear Name we raise
    With one accord our parting hymn of praise ;
  We stand to bless Thee ere our worship cease,
  Then, lowly kneeling, wait Thy word of peace.

2 Grant us Thy peace upon our homeward way ;
  With Thee began, with Thee shall end the day ;

Guard Thou the lips from sin, the hearts from shame,
That in this house have called upon Thy Name.

3 Grant us Thy peace, Lord, through the coming night,
Turn Thou for us its darkness into light ;
From harm and danger keep Thy children free,
For dark and light are both alike to Thee.

4 Grant us Thy peace throughout our earthly life,
Our balm in sorrow, and our stay in strife ;
Then, when Thy voice shall bid our conflict cease,
Call us, O Lord, to Thine eternal peace.

Amen.

GLORIA PATRI.

1.

L. M.

PRAISE God from Whom all blessings flow ;
Praise Him all creatures here below ;
Praise Him above, ye heavenly host ;
Praise Father, Son, and Holy Ghost.   Amen

2.

L. M.

TO Father, Son, and Holy Ghost,
The God Whom earth and heaven adore,
Be glory, as it was of old,
Is now, and shall be evermore.   Amen

3.   *C. M.*

TO Father, Son, and Holy Ghost,
   The God Whom we adore,
Be glory, as it was, is now,
   And shall be evermore.   AMEN.

4.   *D. C. M.*

TO praise the Father, and the Son,
   And Spirit all-divine,—
The One in Three, and Three in One,—
   Let saints and angels join ;—
Glory to Thee, bless'd Three in One,
   The God Whom we adore,
As was, and is, and shall be done,
   When time shall be no more.   AMEN.

5.   *S. M.*

TO God the Father, Son,
   And Spirit, glory be,
As 't was, and is, and shall be so
   To all eternity.   AMEN.

6.   *D. S. M.*

PRAISE as in ages past,
   Praise as in glory now,
Praise while eternity shall last,
   To Thee, O God, we bow ;

Whom all the heavenly host
And saints on earth adore;
To Father, Son, and Holy Ghost
Be glory evermore.   AMEN

7   5s. 6s. 5s.

BY angels in heaven
  Of every degree,
And saints upon earth,
  All praise be address'd,
To God in Three Persons,
  One God ever bless'd ;
As it has been, now is,
  And always shall be.   AMEN

8.   6s. 4s.

TO Father and to Son
  And Spirit, Three in One,
    All praise be given,
As hath been heretofore
And shall be evermore :
Let all His Name adore
    In earth and heaven.   AMEN.

9.   6s. 5s.

GLORY to the Father,
  Glory to the Son,
And to Thee, Blest Spirit,
  Whilst all ages run.   AMEN.

10. *6s. 8s.*

TO God the Father, Son,
    And Spirit, ever bless'd,
Eternal Three in One,
    All worship be address'd;
        As heretofore
            It was, is now,
            And shall be so
        For evermore.   AMEN.

11. *7s.*

HOLY Father, Holy Son,
    Holy Spirit, Three in One!
Glory, as of old, to Thee,
Now, and evermore shall be!   AMEN.

12. *Six 7s.*

PRAISE the Name of God most high,
    Praise Him, all below the sky,
Praise Him, all ye heavenly host,
Father, Son, and Holy Ghost;
As through countless ages past,
Evermore His praise shall last.   AMEN.

13. *7s., double.*

HOLY Father, Fount of light,
    God of wisdom, goodness, might;
Holy Son, Who cam'st to dwell,
God with us, Emmanuel;

Holy Spirit, Heavenly Dove,
God of comfort, peace, and love;
Evermore be Thou adored,
Holy, Holy, Holy Lord.   AMEN.

N.B.—For metre Ten 7s. begin this doxology by prefix-
ing the last two lines, thus :—

Holy, Holy, Holy Lord,
Evermore be Thou adored,
Holy Father, etc.

14.   *7s. 6s., double.*

O FATHER ever glorious,
    O everlasting Son,
O Spirit all victorious,
    Thrice Holy Three in One,—
Great God of our salvation,
    Whom earth and heaven adore,
Praise, glory, adoration,
    Be Thine for evermore.   AMEN.

15.   *Six 8s.*

TO God the Father, God the Son,
    And God the Spirit, Three in One,
Be glory in the highest given,
By all in earth, and all in heaven;
As was through ages heretofore,
Is now, and shall be evermore.   AMEN.

16.   *8s. 6.*

O HOLY Father, Holy Son,
  And Holy Spirit, Three in One,
As was, and is, and shall be done,
  Glory to Thee, O Lord.   AMEN

17.   *8s. 6s.*

TO Father, Son, and Holy Ghost,
  The God Whom heaven's triumphant host
And saints on earth adore;
Be glory as in ages past,
As now it is, and so shall last
  When time shall be no more.   AMEN.

18.   *8s. 7s.*

PRAISE the Father, earth and heaven,
  Praise the Son, the Spirit praise;
As it was, and is, be given
  Glory through eternal days.   AMEN.

19.   *8s. 7s.. double.*

LEt the voice of all creation,
Earth and heaven's triumphant host,
Praise the God of our salvation,
  Father, Son, and Holy Ghost.
See the heavenly elders casting
  Golden crowns before His throne :
Hallelujahs everlasting
  Be to Him, and Him alone.   AMEN.

20. 8s. 7s. 4.

GREAT Jehovah ! we adore Thee,
  God the Father, God the Son,
God the Spirit, join'd in glory
  On the same eternal throne :
    Endless praises
  To Jehovah, Three in One.   AMEN.

21. 8s. 7s. 7s.

TO the Father, throned in heaven,
  To the Saviour, Christ, His Son,
To the Spirit, praise be given,
  Everlasting Three in One :
As of old, the Trinity
Still is worshipped, still shall be.   AMEN.

22. 10s.

TO God the Father, and to God the Son,
  To God the Holy Spirit, Three in One,
Be praise from all on earth and all in heaven,
As was, and is, and ever shall be given.   AMEN.

23. 11s.

O FATHER, Almighty, to Thee be address'd,
  With Christ and the Spirit, One God ever
    bless'd,

All glory and worship from earth and from
    heaven,
As was, and is now, and shall ever be given.

AMEN.

24.

COME, let us adore Him ; come, bow at His
    feet ;
O give Him the glory, the praise that is meet ;
Let joyful hosannas unceasing arise,
And join the full chorus that gladdens the skies.

AMEN.

THE END.

INDEX OF REFERENCE.

The last column refers to the number of the *hymn* in the musical editions of the "Church Hymnal," the "Parish Hymnal," and "The Supplement ;" to the number of the *page* in all the other books. The *page* numbers are italicized.

No.	First line.	Metre and Tune.	Music found in.	No.
1	Lo ! He comes with clouds descending	8s. 7s. 4. St. Peter's Westminster.	Hall & Whitely.	1
2	When He cometh, when He cometh		Fresh Laurels.	*65*
			Songs of Gladness..	*16*
			Songs of Salvation.	*91*
3	Watchman, tell us of the night	7s., *double.* Watchman (Mason's).	Goodrich & Gilbert	43
			Chant and Tune-Book.	(2) *61*
			Hollister.	*17*
			Happy Voices.	*54*
4	Hark ! the glad sound, the Saviour comes	C. M. Antioch.	Hosanna.	*140*
			Happy Voices.	*118*
5	Hail, Thou long expected Jesus	8s. 7s. Saxony.	Chant and Tune-Book.	*99*
6	Shout the glad tidings, exultingly sing	Avison.	Chant and Tune-Book.	*146*
			Songs of Salvation.	*134*
			Tune-Book.	*320*
7	While shepherds watch-'d their flocks by night	C. M. Shepherds.	Chant and Tune-Book.	*62*

No.	First line.	Metre and Tune.	Music found in.	No.
8	Ye angels in glory	Chorus of Fire	Fresh Laurels.	110
9	Silent night! holy night!		Hollister.	84
10	Wonderful night! wonderful night!		S. S. Chant and Tune-Book.	143
11	Christ is born and heaven rejoices		Happy Voice	153
12	The city's hum was hush'd and still		Happy Voices.	160
13	O come all ye faithful	Adeste Fidelis.	Hall & Whitely.	19
			Hutchins.	19
			Goodrich & Gilbert	19
			Hosanna.	115
			Happy Voices.	45
14	Angels from the realms of glory	8s. 7s. 4. Gilbert's.	Goodrich & Gilbert	24
			Hutchins. (1)	24
15	Hail to the Lord's Anointed	7s. 6s., *double.* Romaine.	Hall & Whitely.	219
			Goodrich & Gilbert	34
			Tune-Book.	268
16	In the wintry heaven	6s. 5s. *double.*	Parish Hymnal.	223
17	Saw ye never in the twilight	8s. 7s. *double.*	Parish Hymnal.	225
18	As with gladness men of old	*Six 7s.* Dix.	Hall & Whitely.	45
			Goodrich & Gilber	45
			Hutchins.	45
			Parish Hymnal.	43

No.	First line.	Metre and Tune.	Music found in.	No.
30	When His salvation bringing	7s. 6s., *double.* Endsleigh.	Hall & Whitely.	175
31	Blessed is He that cometh		Chaplet.	3
32	Hail, Thou once despisèd Jesus	8s. 7s., *double.* Autumn.	Bradbury Trio. Fresh Laurels. Happy Voices. Songs of Salvation.	81 59 190 112
33	Light and comfort of my soul	7s.	Fresh Laurels.	35
34	When I survey the wondrous cross	*L. M.* Federal Street	Hall & Whitely. Chant and Tune-Book.	57 77
35	Day of wonder, day of gladness	8s. 7s., *double.*	Parish Hymnal.	226
36	Jesus lives ! no longer now	St. Albinus.	Hall & Whitely. Goodrich & Gilbert Hutchins. Parish Hymnal.	104 104 104 78
37	Put on, put on your best array		Parish Hymnal.	227
38	Christ the Lord is risen to-day	7s. Easter Hymn.	Hall & Whitely. Goodrich & Gilbert Hutchins. Parish Hymnal. Chant and Tune-Book.	99 99 98 79 79
39	Christ hath arisen		S. S. Chant and Tune-Book. Hollister.	164 54

No.	First line.	Metre and Tune.	Music found in.	No.
40	How in the flowery spring, my God	8s. 6s. *double.*	Hollister.	48
41	He is risen, He is not here		Happy Voices.	164
42	Children, come, and we'll sing the wonderful love	Wonderful Tree.	Songs of Gladness..	159
43	Christ is risen ! Christ is risen !		Chaplet.	50
44	Christ is risen ! Christ is risen !		Supplement.	2
45	Who is He in yonder stall		Songs of Gladness. Songs of Salvation.	162 111
46	See ! the conqueror mounts in triumph	8s. 7s., *double.* Rex Gloriæ	Parish Hymnal.	81
47	Look, ye saints ! the sight is glorious	8s. 7s. 4. Diadem.	Goodrich & Gilbert	115
48	Our Lord is risen from the dead	*L. M., Triple.* Schumann.	Supplement.	3
49	He's come ! let every knee be bent	*C. M.* Chesterfield.	Hall & Whitely. Goodrich & Gilbert	365 15
50	Come, Holy Spirit, Heavenly Dove	*C. M.* (1) Alexandria (2) Balerma.	Goodrich & Gilbert Hall & Whitely. (1) Hutchins. Goodrich & Gilbert Bradbury Trio.	128 460 222 222 123
51	O Spirit of the living God	*L. M.,* Mendon (German Air.)	Hall & Whitely. Hutchins. Ch'nt & Tune-Book Tune-Book.	192 408 83 154

No.	First line.	Metre and Tune.	Music found in.	No.
52	Holy, holy, holy! Lord God Almighty!	Nicæa.	Hall & Whitely.	138
			Goodrich & Gilbert	138
			Hutchins.	138
			Parish Hymnal.	92
53	Holy Father! hear my cry	7s. Nuremberg.	Goodrich & Gilbert	373
			Hutchins.	220
			Bradbury Trio.	319
			Tune-Book.	280
54	Come, Thou Almighty King	6s. 4s. Italian Hymn.	Hall & Whitely.	428
			Goodrich & Gilbert	428
			Hutchins.	428
			Parish Hymnal.	106
			Chant and Tune-Book.	134
55	We give immortal praise	6s. 8s. Darwell.	Hall & Whitely.	143
			Goodrich & Gilbert	307
			Hutchins.	152
			Chant and Tune-Book.	106
			Tune-Book.	260
56	Glory to the Father give	7s. *with chor.* Mozart.	Chant and Tune-Book.	42
57	To Thy temple I repair	7s. Horton.	Ch'nt & Tune-Book	58
58	Sweet the Sabbath morning		Fresh Laurels.	47
59	O day of rest and gladness	7s. 6s., *double.* (1) Hodnet.	Gretorex.	104
		(2) Hodges.	Parish Hymnal.	18
61	The strain upraise of joy and praise	Troyte.	Hall & Whitely. (1)	425
			Goodrich & Gilbert	425
			Hutchins.	425
			Parish Hymnal.	173

No.	First line.	Metre and Tune.	Music found in.	No.
60	The field bedecked with flowers	7s. 6s., *double.*	Hollister, Supplement.	56
62	O worship the King	5s. 6s. 5s. Lyons.	Hall & Whitely. Goodrich & Gilbert Chant and Tune-Book. Hosanna.	406 35 101 41
63	The Lord my pasture shall prepare	*Six* 8s. Creation.	Songs of Gladness. Songs of Salvation.	172 88
64	He leadeth me! O blessed thought		Supplement.	4
65	God shall charge His angel legions	8s. 7s. Wilmot	Chant and Tune-Book.	43
66	Guide me, O Thou great Jehovah	8s. 7s. 4. (1) Oliphant. (2) Autumn.	Hosanna. Bradbury Trio. Fresh Laurels. Happy Voices. Songs of Salvation.	128 81 59 190 112
67	God of our Fathers, by Whose hand	C. M. Warwick.	Hall & Whitely. Songs of Gladness. Tune-Book.	154 114 126
68	Through all the changing scenes of life	C. M. (1) St. Martin's (2) Coronation	Hall & Whitely. Hutchins. (2) Chant and Tune-Book. Bradbury Trio.	322 424 46 179
69	Through the day so rosy bright		Chaplet.	19
70	Jesus is our loving Saviour	8s. 7s. 4.	Fresh Laurels.	4

No.	First line.	Metre and Tune.	Music found in.	No,
71	Salvation, O the joyful sound	*C. M., with chorus.* Ashley.	Hall & Whitely. Tune-Book.	369 132
72	To our Redeemer's glorious Name	*C. M.* Henry.	Chant and Tune-Book.	49
73	For ever here my rest shall be	*C. M.* Cowper.	Hollister. Hosanna.	122 112
74	The voice of free grace	Scotland.	Ch. and Tune-Book	55
75	Blow ye the trumpet, blow	*6s. 8s.* (1) Lenox. (2) Darwell.	S. S. Chant and Tune-Book. Bradbury Trio. Hosanna. Fresh Laurels. Hall & Whitely. Hutchins. Goodrich & Gilbert Tune-Book. S. S. Chant and Tune-Book.	100 369 111 66 143 152 307 200 106
76	O Word of God incarnate	*7s. 6s., double.* Lancashire.	Hall & Whitely. Hutchins.	362 10
77	The Bible! the Bible more precious than gold	*11s.*	Hosanna. Fresh Laurels. Oriola.	16 89 131
78	I love Thy kingdom, Lord	*S. M.* Laban.	Hall & Whitely. Chant and Tune-Book. Bradbury Trio. Fresh Laurels.	170 56 61 43
79	Glorious things of Thee are spoken	*8s. 7s., double.* Austria.	Hall & Whitely. Goodrich & Gilbert Hutchins.	190 190 190

No.	First line.	Metre and Tune.	Music found in.	N(
80	When of old the Jewish mothers	8s. 7s. 4.	Parish Hymnal.	15
81	In token that thou shalt not fear	C.M. Manoah	Hall & Whitely.	5
82	Jesus, and shall it ever be	L.M. (1) Russian Hymn. (2) Melcombe.	Supplement. Goodrich & Gilbert	1 12
83	Remember thy Creator now	Rose of Sharon.	Happy Voices.	5
84	Go thou in life's fair morning	7s. 6s., *with chorus.*	Supplement.	
85	O won't you be a Christian		Happy Voices.	3
86	The Master is coming, He calleth for thee	11s., *with chorus.*	Songs of Salvation.	2
87	The Spirit in our hearts	S. M. Shirland.	Goodrich & Gilbert Hosanna.	24 13
88	O happy is the man who hears	C.M. Chimes	Ch'nt & Tune-Book	7
89	My Saviour stands waiting, and knocks at the door	Let the good angels come in.	Fresh Laurels.	12
90	Just as I am, without one plea	8s. 6s. (1) Howard. (2) St. Crispin.	Hall & Whitely. (2) Goodrich & Gilb.(2) Parish Hymnal. (1)	39 39 6
91	O Jesu, Thou art standing	7s. 6s., *double.* Aurelia.	Hall & Whitely. Hutchins.	1 20

No.	First line.	Metre and Tune.	Music found in.	No.
92	What shall I do with Jesus	7s. 6s., *double.*	Supplement.	6
93	Jesu, lover of my soul	7s., *double.* St. George's.	Hall & Whitely. Hutchins. (2) Goodrich & Gilb.(1)	42 100 306
94	Rock of Ages! cleft for me	*Six 7s.* (1) Redhead 76. (2) Who is He	Hall & Whitely. Hutchins. (1) Goodrich & Gilbert Songs of Gladness. Songs of Salvation.	391 391 391 162 111
95	Awake, my soul, stretch every nerve	C. M. Christmas.	Hall & Whitely. Hutchins.	476 476
96	Rise, my soul, and stretch thy wings	7s. 6s., *double.* Amsterdam.	Hall & Whitely. Goodrich & Gilbert Hollister. Hosanna.	447 447 126 78
97	Prayer is the soul's sincere desire	C. M. Burlington.	Hall & Whitely. Hutchins. Tune-Book.	203 415 56
98	Go, when the morning shineth	7s. 6s., *double, with chorus.*	Supplement.	5
99	Our Father who art in heaven		Supplement.	7
100	All hail the power of Jesus' Name	C. M. Miles' Lane.	Hall & Whitely. Goodrich & Gilbert Hutchins. (1) Parish Hymnal.	424 424 424 137

No.	First line.	Metre and Tune.	Music found in.	No.
101	How sweet the Name of Jesus sounds	*C. M.*, *with chorus.* Who 's like Jesus.	Supplement.	14
102	The valleys and the mountains		Happy Voices.	13
103	Songs of praise the angels sang	*7s.*, *with chorus.* Mozart.	Chant and Tune-Book.	42
104	Saviour, blessèd Saviour	*6s. 5s.*, *double.* St. John.	Parish Hymnal.	101
105	We praise Thee, we bless Thee		Fresh Laurels.	104
106	God, my King, Thy might confessing	*8s. 7s.*) (1) Rathbun. (2) Star of Bethlehem.	Hall & Whitely. Happy Voices.	423 159
107	Lord, with glowing heart I 'd praise Thee	*8s. 7s.*, *double.* Rapture.	Hutchins. (1) Tune-Book.	494 284
108	Saviour, source of every blessing	*8s. 7s.*, *with chorus.* Russian Air.	Parish Hymnal. Chant and Tune-Book.	12 115
109	O bless the Lord, my soul	*S. M.* Meade.	Ch'nt & Tune-Book	97
110	Work, for the night is coming		Bradbury Trio. Songs of Gladness.	194 17
111	If you cannot on the ocean	*8s, 7s. double.*	Supplement.	8
112	In the vineyard of our Father	*8s. 7s. 4.* Mabel.	Hutchins. Parish Hymnal.	227 154

No.	First line.	Metre and Tune.	Music found in.	No.
113	Fight the good fight bravely	6s. 5s., *double, with chorus.*	Chaplet.	13
114	Am I a soldier of the cross	C. M. Azmon.	Chant and Tune-Book.	131
			Hosanna.	134
			Songs of Salvation.	105
115	Soldiers of Christ, arise	S. M. Silver Street.	Hall & Whitely.	216
			Goodrich & Gilbert	216
			Hutchins.	216
			Chant and Tune-Book.	116
			Bradbury Trio.	214
116	Sound the battle-cry		Echo to Happy Voices.	75
117	Nearer, my God, to Thee	(1) Horbury. (2) Bethany.	Hall & Whitely. (1)	507
			Hall & Whitely. (2)	507
			Goodrich & Gilb. (1)	507
			Bradbury Trio.	77
			Hollister.	73
118	O Lord, young martyrs brave and true	L. M. Truro.	Hall & Whitely.	117
			Goodrich & Gilbert	120
			Hutchins.	301
			Tune-Book.	198
119	My Father, I would be Thy child		Bradbury Trio.	333
120	God has said, forever blessèd	8s. 7s. 4. Zion.	S. S. Chant and Tune-Book.	59
			Hosanna.	127
121	Lead us, Heavenly Father, lead us	8s. 7s. 4. Gilbert's.	Goodrich & Gilbert	505
			Hutchins. (1)	24

No.	First line.	Metre and Tune.	Music found in.	No.
122	Thou art the way, to Thee alone	*C. M.* (1) Swanwick. (2) Downs.	Tune-Book. Hall & Whitely.	116 214
123	Breast the wave, Christian	Schell.	Hall & Whitely.	172
124	Jesus, my strength, my hope	*D. S. M.* Dennis.	Ch'nt & Tune-Book Bradbury Trio. Hosanna. Happy Voices.	44 225 105 117
125	Words are things of little cost	*Six 7s.* Dix.	Hall & Whitely. Goodrich & Gilbert Hutchins. Parish Hymnal.	45 45 45 43
126	I was a wandering sheep	*D. S. M.* Lebanon.	S. S. Chant and Tune-Book. Hollister, Supple'nt Happy Voices.	53 49 45
127	Saviour, like a shepherd	8s. 7s. 4.	Chant and Tune-Book. Bradbury Trio.	118 94
128	Sitting at the feet of Jesus	8s. 7s., *double.*	Songs of Gladness.	8
129	I lay my sins on Jesus	7s. 6s., *double.* Mendelssohn.	Supplement.	9
130	Art thou weary, art thou languid	St. Stephen the Sabaite.	Hutchins.	514
131	Children of the heavenly King	7s. Pleyel's Hymn.	Hall & Whitely. Goodrich & Gilb.(2) Hutchins. Parish Hymnal. Ch'nt & Tune-Book	449 477 449 150 41

No.	First line.	Metre and Tune.	Music found in.	No.
132	Those eternal bowers	6s. 5s., *double.* St. John.	Parish Hymnal.	101
133	Stand up, stand up for Jesus	7s. 6s., *double*, Webb.	Bradbury Trio. Hosanna. Songs of Salvation. Oriola.	104 101 25 84
134	Lord, forever at Thy side	7s. Weber.	Hall & Whitely. Hutchins. (1)	406 406
135	The Son of God goes forth to war	D. C. M. (1) Hollandish Air. (2) Old 81st.	Supplement. Hall & Whitely. Hutchins.	17 176 176
136	My faith looks up to Thee	6s. 4s. Olivet.	Hall & Whitely. (1) Happy Voices. Fresh Laurels. Songs of Salvation.	237 41 83 89
137	I heard the voice of Jesus say	D. C. M. Brattle Street.	Goodrich & Gilbert	441
138	Once in royal David's city	8s. 7s. 7s. Unscher Hernscher.	Goodrich & Gilbert	107
139	How firm a foundation, ye saints of the Lord	11s. Hinton.	Chant and Tune-Book.	47
140	A charge to keep I have	S. M. (1) Leighton. (2) Boylston.	Hall & Whitely. (1) Hall & Whitely. Goodrich & Gilbert Bradbury Trio. Songs of Gladness.	489 315 315 325 110
141	God of mercy throned on high	7s. Herold.	S. S. Chant and Tune-Book.	93

No.	First line.	Metre and Tune.	Music found in.	No.
142	Lord, I hear of showers of blessing	8s. 7s. 4. Even me.	Bradbury Trio. Hosanna.	209 172
143	Hark! hark, my soul! Angelic songs are swelling!	(1) Angels of Jesus. (2) Vox An-gelica.	Parish Hymnal. (3) Goodrich & Gilb.(2 Hall & Whitely. Hutchins. (1) Parish Hymnal. (1)	185 485 485 485 185
144	Brief life is here our portion	7s. 6s., *double.* Aurelia.	Hall & Whitely. Hutchins.	10 202
145	Jerusalem the golden	7s. 6s., *double.* Ewing.	Hall & Whitely. Hutchins. Parish Hymnal. Ch. and Tune-Book Songs of Gladness..	493 493 186 68 46
146	Come, Lord, and warm each languid heart	C. M., *with chorus.* Welcome Home.	Songs of Gladness. Songs of Salvation.	147 182
147	Come, we that love the Lord	S. M., *with chorus.* We'll be there.	Supplement.	16
148	O Paradise, O Paradise	Paradise (Barnby).	Hutchins. (2) Parish Hymnal. (2)	509 187
149	Beautiful mansions, Home of the blest	Beautiful Mansions.	Fresh Laurels.	9
150	There's a home of joy unfading	8s. 7s., *double, with chorus.* Gates Ajar.	Supplement.	10
151	In the far better land of glory and light	11s., *with chorus.* Hallelujah.	Happy Voices.	10

No.	First line.	Metre and Tune.	Music found in.	No.
152	All praise to Thee, Who safe hast kept	*L. M.* (1) Stonefield. (2) Wellington	Hall & Whitely. Goodrich & Gilbert Tune-Book. Gretorex.	235 407 190 59
153	Sun of my soul, Thou Saviour dear	*L. M.* Hursley	Hall & Whitely. Goodrich & Gilbert Hutchins. (1) Parish Hymnal.	336 336 336 3
154	Abide with me; fast falls the eventide	10*s.* Eventide	Hall & Whitely. (1) Goodrich & Gilbert Hutchins. (1) Parish Hymnal. Songs of Glad'ss (2)	335 335 335 9 64
155	Softly now the light of day	7*s.* Solitude.	Hall & Whitely.	445
156	All praise to Thee, my God, this night	*L. M.* Tallis.	Hall & Whitely. Goodrich & Gilbert Hutchins. Parish Hymnal.	333 333 333 7
157	Thou, Whose almighty word	6*s.* 4*s.* Italian Hymn. (Moscow).	Hall & Whitely. Goodrich & Gilbert Hutchins. Parish Hymnal. Chant and Tune-Book.	492 428 428 106 134
158	Fling out the banner! let it float	*L. M.* St. Helena.	Parish Hymnal.	110
159	Lord, our offerings we are bringing	8*s.* 7*s.*, *double.* (1) Frederick. (2) Harwell.	Tune-Book. Ch. & Tune-Book. Hosanna. Fresh Laurels.	295 78 122 57

No.	First line.	Metre and Tune.	Music found in.	No.
160	The morning light is breaking	7s. 6s., *double.* Webb.	Bradbury Trio. Hosanna. Songs of Salvation. Oriola.	104 101 25 84
161	From Greenland's icy mountains	7s. 6s., *double.* Missionary Hymn.	Hall & Whitely. (1) Goodrich & Gilbert Hutchins. (1) Chant and Tune-Book. Hosanna.	283 283 283 87 119
162	Jesus shall reign where-e'er the sun	L. M. Missionary Chant.	Hall & Whitely. Goodrich & Gilbert Hutchins. Songs of Gladness	290 273 290 127
163	Peacefully lay her down to sleep		Bradbury Trio.	24
164	Asleep in Jesus! blessèd sleep	L. M. Rest.	Hall & Whitely.	260
165	Brightly gleams our banner	6s. 5s., *double.*	Hutchins. (2) Parish Hymnal.	232 210
166	Onward, Christian soldiers	6s. 5s., *double.* Onward.	Goodrich & Gilb.(1) Hutchins. (1) Parish Hymnal. (1)	232 232 208
167	Marching on! marching on! glad as birds on the wing		Happy Voices. Songs of Gladness.	139 31
168	Come with singing		Songs of Salvation.	28
169	My country 't is of thee	6s. 4s. America.	Hall & Whitely. Goodrich & Gilbert Bradbury Trio. Hollister.	309 309 103 146

233